Achieving your TAQA Assessor and Internal Quality Assurer Award

Achieving your TAQA Assessor and Internal Quality Assurer Award

Ann Gravells

Los Angeles | London | New Delhi
Singapore | Washington DC

Learning Matters
An imprint of SAGE Publications Ltd
1 Oliver's Yard
55 City Road
London EC1Y 1SP

SAGE Publications Inc.
2455 Teller Road
Thousand Oaks, California 91320

SAGE Publications India Pvt Ltd
B 1/I 1 Mohan Cooperative Industrial Area
Mathura Road
New Delhi 110 044

SAGE Publications Asia-Pacific Pte Ltd
3 Church Street
#10–04 Samsung Hub
Singapore 049483

Editor: Amy Thornton
Development editor: Jennifer Clark
Production controller: Chris Marke
Project management: Deer Park Productions,
Tavistock, Devon
Marketing manager: Zoe Seaton
Typeset by: Pantek Media, Maidstone, Kent
Printed by: MPG Printgroup, UK

Library of Congress Control Number:
2011944211

British Library Cataloguing in Publication Data
A catalogue record for this book is available from
the British Library

ISBN: 978 0 85725 717 8

MIX
Paper from
responsible sources
FSC
www.fsc.org   FSC® C018575

CONTENTS

ACKNOWLEDGEMENTS

I would like to thank the following for their support and contributions while working on this book: Angela Faulkener, Angela O'Leary, Bob Freeman, Johanna Hurren, Gaynor Mount, Gill Payne, Jacklyn Williams, Joan Willison, Marie Faulkner, Mel Page, Peter Adeney, Sue Mullins, Suzanne Blake and Vickie Prince.

I would also like to thank my father Bob Gravells for his excellent proofreading skills – even though he knew nothing about assessment when he started, he certainly does now. Also, my husband Peter Frankish who never complains about the amount of time I spend in the office and makes endless cups of tea to keep me going. Thanks also to Jennifer Clark, and Amy Thornton from Learning Matters, who are always at the end of the phone when I feel under pressure and need motivation and encouragement.

Thanks also go to the staff and learners of the teacher training department at Bishop Burton College, who always inspire me.

Every effort has been made to trace the copyright holders and to obtain their permission for the use of copyright material. The publisher and author will gladly receive any information enabling them to rectify any error or omission in subsequent editions.

Ann Gravells
www.anngravells.co.uk
January 2012

Ann Gravells is a lecturer in teacher training at Bishop Burton College in East Yorkshire and a consultant to the University of Cambridge's Institute of Continuing Education's Assessment Network. She has been teaching since 1983.

Ann is a director of her own company *Ann Gravells Ltd*, an educational consultancy which specialises in teaching, training and quality assurance. She delivers events and courses nationwide.

Ann holds a Masters in Educational Management, a PGCE, a Degree in Education, and a City & Guilds Medal of Excellence for teaching. Ann is a Fellow of the Institute for Learning and holds QTLS status.

She is often asked how her surname should be pronounced. The 'vells' part of Gravells is pronounced like 'bells'.

Ann is the author of the following Learning Matters books:

- *Achieving your TAQA Assessor and Internal Quality Assurer Award*
- *Delivering Employability Skills in the Lifelong Learning Sector*
- *Passing PTLLS Assessments*
- *Preparing to Teach in the Lifelong Learning Sector*
- *Principles and Practice of Assessment in the Lifelong Learning Sector*
- *What is Teaching in the Lifelong Learning Sector?*

Co-author of:

- *Equality and Diversity in the Lifelong Learning Sector*
- *Passing CTLLS Assessments*
- *Planning and Enabling Learning in the Lifelong Learning Sector*

Edited:

- *Study Skills for PTLLS*

The author welcomes any comments from readers; please contact her via her website.

www.anngravells.co.uk

In this chapter you will learn about:

- the structure of the book and how to use it
- TAQA qualifications
- how to achieve your TAQA Award
- Qualifications and Credit Framework (QCF)
- Lifelong Learning Professional Teaching Standards

The structure of the book and how to use it

Welcome to the roles of assessment and internal quality assurance. Whether you are a new or an experienced practitioner, this book will guide you through the terminology, processes and practices to enable you to improve your role and/or work towards a relevant qualification.

The book has been specifically written for assessors and internal quality assurers who are working towards the Training, Assessment and Quality Assurance Awards and Certificates (TAQA). The content is also applicable to anyone requiring further information to assist their job role, or for continuing professional development (CPD).

Due to the terminology used throughout the subject areas, you will find lots of acronyms within the book. The first occurrence of the word in each chapter will always be in full, with the acronym in brackets. The acronym will then be used throughout the rest of the chapter. A list of the most commonly used ones can be found at the end of this chapter.

The book is also relevant to units from the:

- Award in Preparing to Teach in the Lifelong Learning Sector (PTLLS)
- Certificate in Teaching in the Lifelong Learning Sector (CTLLS)
- Diploma in Teaching in the Lifelong Learning Sector (DTLLS).

The book is structured in chapters which relate to the content of the three assessment and three internal quality assurance (IQA) units. You can work logically through the chapters or just look up relevant aspects which relate to the units you are working towards. Some aspects within one unit might also be applicable to another unit. Therefore, rather than duplicate text, there will be a statement referring you to a particular chapter for more information.

There are activities and examples within each chapter which will assist your understanding of the assessment and IQA process. At the end of each chapter section is an extension activity to stretch and challenge your learning further. If you are working towards a TAQA unit, completing the activities will help you to gather suitable evidence. At the end of each chapter is a list of possible evidence which could be used towards your achievement of the TAQA unit.

A cross-referencing grid at the end of each chapter shows how the content contributes towards the TAQA units' assessment criteria. There is also a theory focus with relevant references, further information and websites that you might like to refer to.

Throughout the chapters there are sample pro-formas and templates that could be used or adapted for assessment and internal quality assurance purposes. However, do check with your organisation in case they have particular documents they require you to use.

Chapter 6 relates to the management of others and as such contains various leadership, management and communication theories.

The appendices contain the learning outcomes and assessment criteria for the TAQA Assessment and Internal Quality Assurance units. These can be used as a checklist towards your progress and achievement.

The index will help you to quickly locate useful topics within the book.

TAQA qualifications

The assessment and internal quality assurance units form part of the Training, Assessment and Quality Assurance (TAQA) suite of qualifications for England, Wales and Northern Ireland; separate standards are available in Scotland.

The units are suitable for anyone assessing or internally quality assuring qualifications, programmes of learning, or competence in the work environment. If you are assessing qualifications which are classed as National Vocational Qualifications (NVQs) it is mandatory that you achieve an Assessor or IQA Award within a given time period. You can take the units whether you are employed full time, part time, are voluntary or peripatetic (working for several organisations).

The qualifications are made up of a combination of units according to assessment or IQA job roles. There is a *knowledge* unit, which can be taken whether you are performing the job role or not, and then one or two *performance* units depending upon the specific requirements of your job role.

The qualifications are based on standards which have been produced by a Sector Skills Council (SSC). These are known as National Occupational Standards (NOS) and should exist for every subject area. SSCs aim to increase the skills and productivity of their sector's workforce and influence the development of qualifications and apprenticeships. They have a major impact on the delivery of publicly and privately funded training throughout the United Kingdom. There will be a SSC, or a similar Standard Setting Body (SSB) for your subject area. It would be useful to find out who they are as they create the assessment strategy/assessment guidance (i.e. requirements for assessors and IQAs) on which the qualification you assess will be based. The SSC for TAQA is the Learning and Skills Improvement Service (LSIS). Once you know who your SSC/SSB is, have a look at their website as you will find lots of useful information regarding your subject.

Once the standards have been approved, an awarding organisation will turn them into qualifications. Any organisation which is approved by them can apply to deliver the accredited qualifications. Your role will be to assess or quality assure the qualification. Several different awarding organisations can offer the same qualification, for example City & Guilds and Edexcel. The qualification content will be the same, but the way it is assessed might differ.

Assessment qualifications

There are three units at level 3; the first is knowledge based and the other two are performance based (see Appendices 1, 2 and 3). As the first unit (Unit 1) is purely knowledge based, it can be taken prior to, or at the same time as, the performance unit. It is ideal for anyone wanting to know what it's like to be an assessor. The units can be achieved in any order and each has a credit value on the Qualifications and Credit Framework (QCF).

1 **Understanding the principles and practices of assessment** (3 credits).

This is a knowledge-based unit for new and existing assessors or anyone who wishes to know about the theory of assessment. You do not need to carry out any assessment activities with learners to achieve this unit.

2 **Assess occupational competence in the work environment** (6 credits).

This is a performance unit for anyone who assesses in the work environment using methods such as observations, questions and examining products of work. The assessments might be towards a qualification, or to confirm employees' workplace competence towards their job specification.

3 **Assess vocational skills, knowledge and understanding** (6 credits).

This is a performance unit for anyone who assesses in any environment using methods such as assignments, projects, simulations and tests. The assessments might be towards qualifications or programmes of learning.

Units 1 and 2 will lead to the *Award in Assessing Competence in the Work Environment*; units 1 and 3 will lead to the *Award in Assessing Vocationally Related Achievement*.

If all three units are achieved this will lead to the *Certificate in Assessing Vocational Achievement*.

Internal quality assurance qualifications

There are three units at level 4, the first is knowledge based and the other two are performance based (see Appendices 4, 5 and 6). As the first unit (Unit 4) is purely knowledge based, it can be taken prior to, or at the same time as, the performance unit. It is ideal for anyone wanting to know what it's like to be an internal quality assurer. The units can be achieved in any order and each has a credit value on the QCF.

4 **Understanding the principles and practices of internally assuring the quality of assessment** (6 credits).

This is a knowledge-based unit for new and existing internal quality assurers or anyone who wishes to know about the theory of internal quality assurance. You do not need to carry out any internal quality assurance activities with assessors to achieve this unit.

5 **Internally assure the quality of assessment** (6 credits).

This is a performance unit for anyone who internally quality assures the work of assessors. For example, observing practice, sampling judgements and decisions, supporting and advising assessors. It can be achieved in any environment by internally quality assuring qualifications, programmes of learning or workplace competence.

6 **Plan, allocate and monitor work in own area of responsibility** (5 credits).

This is a performance unit for anyone who leads the internal quality assurance process within an organisation. The role will include having a responsibility for managing the quality and performance of assessors and/or other internal quality assurers. Developing systems and liaising with external inspectors might also be part of this role.

Units 4 and 5 will lead to the *Award in Internally Assuring the Quality of Assessment*; Units 4, 5 and 6 will lead to the *Certificate in Leading the Internal Quality Assurance of Assessment Processes and Practice*.

How to achieve your TAQA Award

First of all, you need to decide which units are relevant to your job role; you can then locate a suitable college or training centre and enrol. It will register you with an awarding organisation, for example, City & Guilds or Edexcel. Awarding organisations have different assessment activities based upon each unit's criteria, for example, an assignment, observation, questions and/or a professional discussion with your assessor. Although the activities may differ depending where you are registered, the content of the units and the assessment criteria remain the same. (See Appendices 1–6).

You could use the Appendices like a checklist to see what you currently know and can already evidence, or what you need to learn and work towards. The two units beginning with the word *understanding* are the knowledge units and can usually be evidenced by an assignment, written statements or a professional discussion. The other units are performance units, which means they have to be evidenced by you actually performing the requirements for real as part of your job role. You can take the units in any order, or at the same time. If it's the latter, your assessor will be able to assess you holistically. This means some aspects evidenced in one unit can be cross-referenced to other relevant units rather than be repeated.

You will be allocated an assessor who will explain how they will assess you, for example, by visiting you in your work environment to observe you in action. You should gather evidence of your achievement in the form of completed assignments, responses to questions and products of your work such as completed assessment or internal quality assurance records. There is guidance at the end of each chapter as to possible evidence you could provide.

You will need to keep all your work in a file or folder, often referred to as a *portfolio*, which can be manual or electronic. Copies of your assessor's records, such as observations and feedback, will also need to be included. If you quote from any textbooks, journals or the internet while producing written work, you will need to reference your work accordingly, otherwise it could be considered as plagiarism. Your assessor should be able to give you advice on the best way to do this.

While you are working towards the units, you might need to be counter-signed by another qualified person in the same subject area as yourself. This is to ensure all your decisions are accurate and that you are carrying out the requirements of the units correctly. How long it takes you to complete will depend upon the time it takes for you to generate all the required evidence. However, you should be given a target date for achievement.

Your work will be assessed and a sample of it might also be internally quality assured during and/or at the end of your programme. When you have passed all the requirements, the college or training centre you have enrolled with will apply for the certificate from the awarding organisation.

Qualifications and Credit Framework (QCF)

Ofqual, together with its partner regulators in Wales (DCELLS) and Northern Ireland (CCEA), is responsible for the regulation of the Qualifications and Credit Framework (QCF). There is a separate framework for Scotland. The frameworks will eventually contain all available qualifications in the country.

The QCF is a system for recognising skills and qualifications by awarding credit values to the units. A credit value of 1 equates to 10 learning hours. These values enable you to see how long it would take an average learner to achieve a unit. For example, the *Understanding the principles and practices of assessment* unit is 3 credits, which equates to 30 hours. The total hours include *contact time* with a teacher and assessor, and *non-contact time* for individual study, assignment work and the production of a portfolio of evidence.

There are three sizes of qualifications with titles and associated credit values:

- Award (1 to 12 credits)
- Certificate (13 to 36 credits)
- Diploma (37 credits or more).

The terms Award, Certificate and Diploma do not relate to progression, i.e. you don't start with an Award, progress to the Certificate and then the Diploma. The terms relate to how big the qualification is (i.e. its size), which is based on the total number of credits. By looking at the title and credit value, you will be able to see how difficult it is and how long it will take to complete.

The difficulty of the qualification is defined by its level. The QCF has 9 levels; entry level plus 1 to 8 (there are 12 levels in Scotland).

A rough comparison of the levels to existing qualifications is:

1 – GCSEs (grades D–G)

2 – GCSEs (grade A*–C)

3 – A levels

4 – Vocational Qualification (VQ) level 4, Higher National Certificate (HNC)

5 – VQ level 5, Degree, Higher National Diploma (HND)

6 – Honours Degree

7 – Masters Degree

8 – Doctor of Philosophy (PhD).

All qualifications on the QCF use the terms *learning outcomes* and *assessment criteria*. The learning outcomes state what the learner *will do*, and the assessment criteria what the learner *can do*. Units are either *knowledge based* (to assess understanding) or *performance based* (to assess competence).

Lifelong Learning Professional Teaching Standards

In September 2007, standards came into effect for all new teachers in the lifelong learning sector who teach or assess on government-funded programmes in England. This includes all post-16 education, including further education, adult and community learning, work-based learning and offender education. Please see the web links at the end of the chapter for Northern Ireland, Scotland and Wales.

The standards encompass six domains:

A Professional Values and Practice

B Learning and Teaching

C Specialist Learning and Teaching

D Planning for Learning

E Assessment for Learning

F Access and Progression.

The domains are broken down into aspects of *scope*, *knowledge* and *practice* which are required in a teaching job role. The full standards can be accessed at the shortcut: http://tinyurl.com/4xkcz5z

If the standards are applicable to your job role, for example, if you are teaching as well as assessing, you will need to achieve a relevant teaching qualification such as the Award in Preparing to Teach in the Lifelong Learning Sector (PTLLS) followed by either the:

- Certificate in Teaching in the Lifelong Learning Sector (CTLLS) if you are an associate teacher *or*

- Diploma in Teaching in the Lifelong Learning Sector (DTLLS) if you are a full teacher.

Some of the TAQA units can be used towards the above qualifications. For example, *Understanding the principles and practices of assessment* is an optional unit in PTLLS. If you achieve the unit before taking PTLLS, it will be classed as Recognition of Prior Learning (RPL) and exempt you from retaking it. You should have been given a Unique Learner Number (ULN, or SCN in Scotland) when you successfully completed the unit and this number will automatically recognise your achievement through the QCF.

For the purpose of the teaching regulations in England, the Institute for Learning's (IfL) definitions of associate and full teacher apply whether you are working on a full-time, part-time, fractional, fixed-term, temporary or agency basis.

The associate teaching role means a teaching role that carries significantly less than the full range of teaching responsibilities and does not require the teacher to demonstrate an extensive range of knowledge, understanding and application of curriculum innovation or curriculum delivery strategies.

The full teaching role means a teaching role that carries the full range of teaching responsibilities and requires the teacher to demonstrate an extensive range of knowledge, understanding and application of curriculum innovation or curriculum delivery strategies.

The Institute for Learning (IfL) is the professional body for teachers, trainers, tutors and trainee teachers in the learning and skills sector in England. If you haven't already done so, you should register with the IfL via their website: www.ifl.ac.uk. The IfL has a *Code of Professional Practice* (2008) for all members to follow.

Acronyms

CCEA	Council for the Curriculum, Examinations and Assessment (Northern Ireland)
CIEA	Chartered Institute of Educational Assessors
COSHH	Control of Substances Hazardous to Health
CPD	Continuing professional development
CTLLS	Certificate in Teaching in the Lifelong Learning Sector
DCELLS	Department for Children, Education, Lifelong Learning and Skills (Wales)
DTLLS	Diploma in Teaching in the Lifelong Learning Sector
DSO	Designated Safeguarding Officer
ECM	Every Child Matters
EDAR	Experience, describe, analyse and revise
EI	Emotional intelligence
EQA	External quality assurer; External quality assurance; External quality assuring
GCSE	General Certificate of Secondary Education
ICT	Information and communication technology
IFL	Institute for Learning
IQ	Intelligence quotient
IQA	Internal quality assurer; Internal quality assurance; Internal quality assuring
NLP	Neuro Linguistic Programming
NOS	National Occupational Standards

NVQ	National Vocational Qualification
Ofqual	Office of Qualifications and Examinations Regulation
Ofsted	Office for Standards in Education, Children's Services and Skills
PPP	Pose, pause, pounce
PTLLS	Preparing to Teach in the Lifelong Learning Sector
QCF	Qualifications and Credit Framework
RARPA	Recognising and recording progress and achievement in non-accredited learning
RPL	Recognition of Prior Learning
RWE	Realistic working environment
SCN	Scottish candidate number
SMART	Specific, measurable, achievable, realistic and time
SQF	Scottish Qualifications Framework
SSB	Standard Setting Body
SSC	Sector Skills Council
SWOT	Strengths, weaknesses, opportunities and threats
TAQA	Training, assessment and quality assurance
ULN	Unique learner number
VACSR	Valid, authentic, current, sufficient and reliable
VARK	Visual, aural, read/write and kinaesthetic
VLE	Virtual learning environment
WWWWWH	Who, what, when, where, why and how

Summary

In this chapter you have learnt about:

- the structure of the book and how to use it
- TAQA qualifications
- how to achieve your TAQA Award
- Qualifications and Credit Framework (QCF)
- Lifelong Learning Professional Teaching Standards.

Theory focus

References and further information

Gravells, A (2012) *Preparing to Teach in the Lifelong Learning* Sector. Exeter: Learning Matters.

IfL (2008) *Code of Professional Practice: Raising concerns about IfL members* (V2). London: Institute for Learning.

LLUK (2006) *New Overarching Professional Standards for Teachers, Tutors and Trainers in the Lifelong Learning Sector.* London: Skills for Business.

Websites

Ann Gravells (information regarding teaching and assessing): www.anngravells. co.uk

CCEA Northern Ireland: www.rewardinglearning.org.uk

City and Guilds: www.cityandguilds.com

DCELLS Wales: www.wales.gov.uk/topics/educationandskills

Edexcel: www.edexcel.com

Further Education Teachers' Qualifications (England) Regulations (2007): www.legislation.gov.uk/uksi/2007/2264/contents/made

Further Education Teachers' Qualifications (Wales): http://tiny.cc/o8who

Institute for Learning: www.ifl.ac.uk

Learning and Skills Improvement Service: www.lsis.org.uk

Ofqual: www.ofqual.gov.uk

Professional Standards for Lecturers in Scotland: http://tiny.cc/3w9jg

Professional Standards for Teachers, Tutors and Trainers in the Lifelong Learning Sector: http://tinyurl.com/4xkcz5z

Qualifications and Credit Framework: http://tinyurl.com/447bgy2

Scottish Credit and Qualifications Framework: www.scqf.org.uk

Sector Skills Councils: www.sscalliance.org

TAQA – Assessing and Assuring the Quality of Assessment: www.excellence-gateway.org.uk/page.aspx?o=283824

Teaching Qualifications for Northern Ireland: http://tiny.cc/2bexb

CHAPTER I
PRINCIPLES AND PRACTICES OF ASSESSMENT

Introduction

In this chapter you will learn about:

- key concepts and principles of assessment
- roles and responsibilities of an assessor
- minimising risks
- types of assessment
- methods of assessment.

There are activities and examples which will help you reflect on the above and will assist your understanding of the principles and practices of assessment. Completing the activities will help you to gather evidence towards the TAQA *Principles and practices of assessment* unit. At the end of each section is an extension activity to stretch and challenge your learning further.

At the end of the chapter is a list of possible evidence which could be used towards the TAQA *Principles and practices of assessment* unit.

A cross-referencing grid shows how the content of this chapter contributes towards the three TAQA units' assessment criteria. There is also a theory focus with relevant references, further information and websites to which you might like to refer.

Key concepts and principles of assessment

Assessment is a way of finding out if learning has taken place. It enables you, as the assessor, to ascertain if your learner has gained the required skills, competence, knowledge, understanding and/or attitudes needed at a given point. It is therefore a process of making a decision regarding your learner's knowledge and/or performance against set criteria. You could be assessing your learners towards a formal qualification, for example an Award, a Certificate or a Diploma in a particular subject. The qualification could be knowledge based, i.e. assessing understanding, or performance based, i.e. assessing practical skills. Alternatively, you might be assessing an employee's competence in the work environment. This might be towards a formal qualification, company standards or to prove they can perform the requirements of their job specification.

Assessment should focus on improving and reinforcing learning as well as measuring achievements. It should help your learners realise how they are progressing and what they need to do to improve and/or progress further.

You might already be assessing groups and/or individuals or you might just want to know what is involved in the assessment process. This chapter will guide you through the knowledge you need to be able to put theory into practice as there are many different methods of assessment which can be used. These will depend on what you are assessing and whether any activities have already been produced for you, for example, observation checklists or assignments. If not, you may have to devise your own.

Activity

Have a look at the TAQA standards in Appendices 1, 2 and 3. Look at the learning outcomes and assessment criteria to see what an assessor should know and do. Appendix 1 relates to knowledge, Appendix 2 to performance (assessing in the work environment) and Appendix 3 to performance (assessing in other contexts).

Assessment is a regular process; it might not always be formalised, but you will be observing what your learners are doing, asking them questions, and reviewing their progress whenever you are in contact with them. If you also teach or train, your learners will be demonstrating their knowledge and skills regularly, for example through activities, discussions and regular tasks. You are therefore constantly making judgements about their progress and how they could improve. You should also be aware of the impact that your comments and grades can have on your learners' confidence when you give them feedback. Comments that specifically focus on the activity or work produced, rather than the individual, will be more helpful and motivating to your learners.

Assessment should not be confused with evaluation; assessment is of the *learner*, evaluation is of the *programme* that the learner is taking, for example, a qualification. Assessment is specific towards learners' achievements and how they can improve. Evaluation is a quality assurance monitoring tool. It includes obtaining feedback from your learners and others, for example, employers, line managers and quality assurers (the revised term for verifiers), to help you improve the overall learner experience as well as your own practice.

There is a difference between assessment *for* learning, and assessment *of* learning. Assessment *for* learning is usually a formative process. It will ascertain progress so far in order to plan further learning and development. Assessment *of* learning is usually summative and confirms that learning has taken place.

Example

Joanna has a new group of learners who are taking an English programme. She asked them to write a short piece of prose and then asked each one to read aloud from a book. This helped Joanna to ascertain the level of her learners' writing, reading and speaking skills. This formative assessment helped her plan an appropriate programme of learning which would lead to a summative examination.

The assessment process is a systematic procedure which should be followed to give your learner a positive experience. Depending upon the subject you are assessing and whether it is academic (theory or knowledge based) or vocational (practical or performance based), you will usually follow the assessment cycle. The cycle will continue until all aspects of the qualification have been successfully achieved by your learner, or they leave the programme. Records must be maintained throughout to satisfy your organisation, the regulatory authorities and awarding organisations.

Figure 1.1 Assessment cycle

- Initial assessment – ascertaining if your learner has any previous knowledge or experience of the subject or topic to be assessed. This information can be obtained through application forms and interviews. The results of initial assessment activities will give you information regarding your learners; for example, any specific assessment require-ments they may have, their learning style or any further training and support they may need. This process might not always be carried out by you, but the information obtained must be passed on to you.

- Assessment planning – agreeing suitable types and methods of assess-ment with each learner, setting appropriate target dates, involving others (such as colleagues or supervisors) as necessary and following relevant organisational guidelines.

- Assessment activity – this relates to the methods used, i.e. assessor led, for example, observation or questioning; or learner led, for exam-ple, completing assignments, writing statements or gathering appropriate evidence of competence. Assessment can be formative (ongoing) and/or summative (at the end).

- Assessment decision and feedback – making a judgement of success or otherwise. Giving constructive feedback and agreeing any further action that may be necessary. Records of what was assessed and the decisions made should always be maintained.

- Review of progress – the assessment plan can be reviewed and updated at any time until your learner completes or decides to leave. Reviewing progress with your learners will give you an opportunity to discuss any other issues that may be relevant to their progress. Reviewing the assessment activities used will give you the opportunity to amend them if necessary.

The cycle will then begin again with an initial assessment regarding the next topic or unit of the qualification. Throughout the cycle, standardisation of assessment practice between assessors should take place; this will help ensure that decisions are consistent and fair and that everyone interprets the requirements in the same way. All assessors should maintain their continual professional development (CPD) and follow legal and organisational requirements. If the qualification is accredited by an awarding organisation, for example, City & Guilds, internal and external quality assurance must take place to ensure assessment is effective.

If you are going to assess accredited qualifications, the starting point should be the programme *syllabus*, often known as a *qualification handbook*. This should state how your subject should be assessed and quality assured. It will give information and guidance in the form of an *assessment strategy*. The assessment strategy should state the experience, professional development and qualifications that assessors and internal quality assurers should hold. It will also state how the subject should be assessed and whether activities are provided for you or you need to create your own.

Activity

Find out who the awarding organisation is for your particular subject and access their website. Locate the qualification handbook and review the assessment strategy to ensure you fulfil it. If you are going to assess accredited or non-accredited programmes of learning, familiarise yourself with what you will assess and how you will do it.

The purpose of the assessment strategy is to ensure the subject is assessed in accordance with relevant guidance and regulations, to give a quality service to your learners, and maintain the reputation of your organisation and the qualification.

If you are going to assess competence and performance in the work environment, the starting point should be the company standards or job specifications. You will need to ensure that they have been written in a way that clearly states what someone has to *know* and what someone has to *do* to achieve the standards. This will help you plan effective activities to assess knowledge and skills.

Try not to be swayed by your own previous experiences of assessment and focus upon the requirement of your learners.

Assessment can be separated into the requirements of the learner, yourself as the assessor, your organisation and the awarding organisation.

Learner – to:	Assessor – to:
• clarify what is expected of them • enable discussions with assessors • evaluate their own progress • have something to show for their achievements, for example a certificate • help them plan and achieve their aim • know how well they are doing • know they are achieving the correct standard or level • know what they have to do to improve and progress further • learn from their mistakes.	• adapt teaching, learning and assessment activities • ascertain learners' progress and achievement so far • carry out all aspects of the assessment cycle and keep records • develop learners' self-assessment skills • diagnose any learner needs or particular learning requirements • empower learners to take control of their learning • follow the requirements of the awarding organisation or company • improve motivation and self-esteem • make decisions and give feedback • prepare learners for further assessments • prove they can assess effectively • standardise judgements and practice with others.
Organisation – to:	**Awarding organisation – to:**
• achieve funding (if applicable) • analyse enrolment, retention, success and achievement rates • ensure adequate resources • ensure consistency of assessors' practice • ensure there is an effective internal quality assurance system • give references for learners if requested • identify gaps in learning • justify delivery of programmes • maintain records • promote a learner-centred approach • satisfy external requirements.	• accredit achievements • ensure compliance with regulations and qualification requirements • ensure staff follow the assessment strategy • give guidance to assessors and internal quality assurers • issue certificates • formulate qualifications from recognised national occupational standards • provide written reports regarding quality and compliance.

Table 1.1: Assessment requirements

Concepts of assessment

Concepts are the aspects involved throughout the assessment process. They include:

- accountability

- achievement

- assessment strategies

- benchmarking

- evaluation

- internally or externally devised assessment methods (formal and informal)

- progression

- transparency

- types of assessment, e.g. initial (at the beginning), formative (ongoing) or summative (at the end).

You need to be *accountable* to your learners and your organisation to ensure you are carrying out your role as an assessor correctly. Your learners should know why they are being assessed and what they have to do to meet the assessment criteria. You will also be accountable to the awarding organisation if you assess their accredited qualifications. You might be accountable to employers if you are assessing their staff in the work environment.

You may be required to analyse *achievement* data and compare this to national or organisational targets. The funding your organisation receives might also be related to your learners' achievements. It's always a useful evaluation method to keep a record of how many learners you have, how many successfully complete their programme and in what timescale.

Following the *assessment strategy* for your subject will ensure you are carrying out your role correctly and holding or working towards the required assessor qualifications.

Benchmarking involves comparing what is the accepted standard for a particular subject area against the current position of your own learners' performance. Using benchmarking data can help inform target setting for individuals or groups. If learners don't achieve the benchmark, an evaluation will need to take place and improvements be implemented. Benchmarking can also be used to compare organisations that provide a similar service, or used within the same organisation to compare performance in different locations.

Evaluation of the assessment process should always take place to inform current and future practice. All aspects of the assessment cycle should be evaluated on an ongoing basis and feedback obtained from all involved.

Internally devised assessments might be produced by you or other staff at your organisation, such as assignments, projects or questions which will also be marked by you. *Externally devised assessments* are usually produced by an awarding organisation, for example, an examination. *Formal* assessments usually count towards achievement of a qualification, whereas *informal* assessments are used to monitor ongoing progress and development.

Progression should be taken into account when assessing learners, i.e. what they are going to do next. It could be another unit of the current qualification, or a different level of qualification, either at your organisation, in the work environment or elsewhere. Progression opportunities should always be discussed with your learner to ensure they are on the right route and that they are capable of achieving.

To assist *transparency*, you need to ensure that everyone who is involved in the assessment process clearly understands what is expected and can see there is nothing untoward taking place. That includes your own interpretation and understanding of the assessment requirements as well as that of your learners. You should be honest with your learners and not let them feel they have achieved more than they are capable of. Auditable records must always be maintained throughout the assessment process.

Types of assessment include initial, formative and summative as well as diagnostic tests which ascertain a learner's current knowledge and experience. Some types of diagnostic tests can also identify learners with dyslexia, dyspraxia, dysgraphia, dyscalculia, etc. Initial assessment is carried out prior to, or at the beginning of, a programme to identify your learner's starting point and level. Formative assessment is ongoing, and summative assessment is at the end.

Principles of assessment

Principles are functions which are based upon the concepts, for example, *how* the assessment process is put into practice.

One important principle is known as VACSR – you need to ensure all assessed work is:

- **V**alid – the work is relevant to the assessment criteria.

- **A**uthentic – the work has been produced solely by the learner.

- **C**urrent – the work is still relevant at the time of assessment.

- **S**ufficient – the work covers all the assessment criteria.

- **R**eliable – the work is consistent across all learners, over time and at the required level.

If the above is not ensured, you might make an incorrect judgement and a learner might appeal against your decision. Conversely, you might not notice a learner has plagiarised someone else's work or done something incorrectly.

Key principles of assessment include:

- communication – this should take place regularly with learners, other assessors, internal quality assurers, employers, etc.

- CPD – maintaining currency of knowledge and skills to ensure your assessment practice and subject knowledge is up to date

- equality and diversity – ensuring all assessment activities embrace equality, inclusivity and diversity and represent all aspects of society

- ethics – ensuring the assessment process is honest and moral, and takes into account confidentiality and integrity

- fairness – assessment activities should be fit for purpose, and planning, decisions and feedback justifiable

- health and safety – ensuring these are taken into account throughout the full assessment process, carrying out risk assessments as necessary

- motivation – encouraging and supporting your learners to reach their maximum potential at an appropriate level

- quality assurance – an integrated process ensuring assessment decisions meet required standards

- record keeping – ensuring accurate records are maintained throughout the teaching, learning and assessment process

- responsibility – making objective decisions, following all organisational guidelines and producing reports as required

- SMART – ensuring all assessment activities are specific, measurable, achievable, realistic and timebound; see Chapter 2 for further details

- standardisation – ensuring the assessment requirements are interpreted accurately and that all assessors are making comparable and consistent decisions.

Quality assurance should be carried out throughout the assessment process. The purpose is to ensure assessors are performing accurately and fairly. Internal quality assurance (IQA) is carried out by a member of staff in the same subject area as the assessors. External quality assurance (EQA) is carried out by a member of the awarding organisation. See Chapter 4 for details of the IQA process and Chapter 5 for the EQA process.

Following the concepts and principles of assessment will ensure you are performing your role as an assessor according to all relevant regulations and requirements.

Extension Activity

Look at the previous bulleted lists of concepts and principles and describe how each will impact upon your role as an assessor. You may need to research some aspects further or speak to relevant staff at your organisation.

Roles and responsibilities of an assessor

Your main role will be to carry out assessments according to the qualification requirements, or those of the programme or job specification. You should have a job description; however, if you don't have one, following the requirements of the TAQA assessor units will ensure you are performing your role adequately. Your roles and responsibilities will include far more than those stated in the assessment cycle on page 15.

For example, your role may involve:

- attending meetings, exhibitions, award ceremonies and presentation events
- checking the authenticity of any witness testimonies
- completing and maintaining safe and secure records
- countersigning other assessors' judgements (if they are not yet qualified)
- dealing with any appeals made against your assessment decisions
- following organisational and regulatory authorities' procedures
- giving constructive and developmental feedback to your learners

- identifying and dealing with any barriers to fair assessment
- implementing internal and external quality assurance action points
- liaising with others involved in the assessment process
- making judgements based on the assessment requirements
- maintaining your own occupational competence and professional development
- negotiating and agreeing assessment plans
- making best use of different assessment types and methods
- providing statistics to managers and others
- reviewing learner progress
- standardising practice with other assessors
- supporting learners with special assessment requirements and dealing with sensitive issues in a supportive manner
- working towards relevant assessment qualifications.

If you are unsure of any aspect of your assessor role, make sure you ask a colleague or your manager. You may be the only assessor for your particular subject within your organisation, therefore it is important that you liaise with your manager or internal quality assurer to ensure you are interpreting the requirements correctly. If you are a member of a team of assessors, you will need to ensure you all work together to give your learners equal and fair access to assessment opportunities. If there are several assessors for the same subject, there will be a co-ordinating or lead assessor who will manage the team and give support and advice regarding the assessment process.

Assessment activities can take place in different environments depending upon what is being assessed and why (see the Example below).

Example

- *Classroom – activities, tests, discussions, role plays, projects, presentations.*
- *Lecture theatre or hall – exams.*
- *Library or home – assignments, research and reading.*
- *Outside environment – practical activities.*
- *Work environment – observations and questions.*
- *Workshop – practical tests and simulations.*

Wherever you are assessing you will need to ensure both you and your learners are suitably prepared, and that you follow the assessment require-ments and relevant organisational and regulatory guidelines.

Your role as an assessor will also be to inspire and motivate your learners. If you are enthusiastic and passionate about your subject, this will help to encourage and challenge your learners. Your learners may already be mo-tivated for personal reasons and be enthusiastic and *want* to perform well. This is known as *intrinsic* motivation. They may be motivated by a *need* to learn, for example to gain a qualification, promotion or pay rise at work, known as *extrinsic* motivation. If you can recognise the difference between your learners' wants and needs, you can appreciate why they are motivated and ensure you make their experience meaningful and relevant. Whatever type of motivation your learners have will be transformed, for better or worse, by what happens during their assessment experience.

There will be certain records and documents that you will need to maintain. These will include assessment plans, feedback records, reviews of progress and overall tracking sheets. Records must be maintained to satisfy organisa-tional and regulatory requirements. You should also safely store confidential documents and audio/digital/video recordings that include learners.

Activity

Find out what documents you need to use to support the assessment process at your organisation. Are they available in hard copy format, or can you access and use them electronically? Explain how each document relates to the various functions of the assessment cycle.

Equality and Diversity

All learners should have equality of opportunity throughout the assess-ment process, providing they are taking a programme they are capable of achieving. There's no point setting learners up to fail, just because you need a certain number of learners for your programme to go ahead, per-haps due to targets or funding. When designing assessment activities, you need to ensure you meet the needs of all your learners and reflect the diverse nature of your group. Never let your own attitudes, values and beliefs interfere with the assessment process. You could design activities which will challenge more able learners and/or promote the motivation of learners who are not progressing so well. You need to differentiate your activities to ensure you are meeting the needs of all your learners, for example, less challenging activities for those who are struggling.

Your organisation will have an Equal Opportunities or Equality and Diversity policy with which you should become familiar. You might have a learner who achieves tasks quickly; having more in-depth and challenging activities available would be beneficial to them. If you have learners who are not achieving the required assessment tasks, you could design an activity that you know they will achieve, to raise their motivation and encourage them to progress further. However, don't oversimplify activities which will leave learners thinking they were too easy. You could always give your learners a choice of, for instance, a straightforward, a challenging or a very challenging activity. Their choice may depend upon their confidence level and you will have to devise such activities beforehand if they are not provided for you. You might need to arrange assessments in other languages, for example Welsh, or use a bilingual approach. If you have different levels of learners within the same group, this can work quite well as they will usually want to attempt something they know they can achieve. However, it can also have the opposite effect in that learners feel they are more capable than they actually are.

Assessment activities should always reflect the diverse nature of your learner group, for example, culture, language and ethnicity. They should not be biased according to the person producing them; otherwise aspects such as terminology or jargon might not be those of the learners, but those of the producer, placing the learner at a disadvantage. You also need to be careful not to discriminate against your learner in any way.

The Equality Act (2010) replaced all previous anti-discrimination legislation and consolidated it into one Act (for England, Scotland and Wales;). It provides rights for people not to be discriminated against or harassed, for example, because they have an association with a disabled person or are wrongly perceived as disabled. In this example, reasonable adjustments must take place during assessment activities to lessen or remove the effects of a disadvantage to a learner with a disability.

The Act contains nine *protected characteristics*:

- age
- disability

- gender

- gender identity

- race

- religion and belief

- sexual orientation

- marriage and civil partnership

- maternity and pregnancy.

There are seven different *types of discrimination.*

1. Associative discrimination: direct discrimination against someone because they are associated with another person with a protected characteristic.

2. Direct discrimination: discrimination because of a protected characteristic.

3. Indirect discrimination: when a rule or policy which applies to everyone can disadvantage a person with a protected characteristic.

4. Discrimination by perception: direct discrimination against someone because others think they have a protected characteristic.

5. Harassment: behaviour deemed offensive by the recipient.

6. Harassment by a third party: the harassment of staff or others by people not directly employed by an organisation, such as an external consultant or visitor.

7. Victimisation: discrimination against someone because they made or supported a complaint under equality legislation.

It is important to take the protected characteristics into account when planning and carrying out assessment activities, and to ensure discrimination does not take place by anyone involved in the assessment process. Try and focus on the positive and always ask what your learner *can do*, not what they *can't do.*

Further details regarding equality and diversity can be found in the companion book *Equality and Diversity in the Lifelong Learning Sector* (Gravells and Simpson, 2012).

Safeguarding

Safeguarding is a term used to refer to the duties and responsibilities that those providing a health, social or education service have to perform to protect individuals and vulnerable people from harm. Following the publication of the Safeguarding Vulnerable Groups Act in 2006, a vetting and barring scheme was established in autumn 2008. This Act created an Independent Barring Board to take all discretionary decisions on whether individuals should be barred from working with children and/or vulnerable adults. As an assessor, you will be bound by this Act if you work with children (those under the age of 18 years in training) and/or vulnerable adults. You will need to attend safeguarding training every three years (some staff every two years depending upon their safeguarding involvement).

A vulnerable adult is defined as *a person aged 18 years or over, who is in receipt of or may be in need of community care services by reason of 'mental or other disability, age or illness and who is or may be unable to take care of him or herself, or unable to protect him or herself against significant harm or exploitation'.* (Bonnerjea, 2009, p9)

This could be anyone needing formal help to live in society, for example, a young mother, someone with a learning disability or a recently released prisoner. If your organisation is inspected by Ofsted, it will be asking your learners how safe they feel and whether they are able to give you feedback regarding any concerns they may have.

You have a duty of care and a personal responsibility towards all your learners and should apply six key elements of appropriate service provision:

- respect
- dignity
- independence
- individuality
- choice
- confidentiality.

There are four key processes that should be followed to ensure your learners are safe:

1. an assessment of their needs

2. planning services to meet these needs

3. intervention if necessary when you have a concern

4. reviewing the services offered.

If you have any concerns regarding a learner, for example, if you feel they are being bullied or may be at risk of harm or abuse, you must refer to your Designated Safeguarding Officer (DSO) immediately. It would be useful to find out who this person is if you don't already know. Never be tempted to get personally involved with your learner's situation.

Every Child Matters (ECM)

The Children Act (2004) provided the legal underpinning for the Every Child Matters: Change for Children programme. The words *learner, adult, citizen* or *person* are often substituted for the word *child* now. Well-being is the term used in the Act to define the five Every Child Matters outcomes. Your organisation might expect you to take these into account when you are in contact with your learners. These are:

- be healthy

- stay safe

- enjoy and achieve

- make a positive contribution

- achieve economic well-being.

Ways to embed the outcomes of Every Child Matters include:

- being healthy – access to drinking water and healthy food, opportunities to keep active

- staying safe – maintaining a safe environment (physical and psychological), health and safety training

- enjoying and achieving – opportunities for all learners to enjoy and achieve a relevant qualification or programme of learning, recognising transferable skills, achieving extra qualifications such as literacy, numeracy and ICT

- making a positive contribution – group activities, role-play and teamwork, citizenship, voluntary work and work experience

- achieving economic well-being – business and enterprise activities, becoming independent and autonomous, gaining employment.

Health and Safety

You will need to follow various regulations: for example, the Health and Safety at Work etc. Act (1974). This places a legal responsibility upon you, as well as your organisation and your learners. If you see a potential hazard, it is your responsibility to do something about it before an accident occurs, even if this is just reporting it to the relevant person within your organisation. The health and safety of yourself, your colleagues and your learners is of paramount importance.

You might have to carry out a risk assessment to ensure the area and assessment activities are safe for all concerned. It can normally be achieved by a walk-through of the area, and a discussion with those involved. However, a formal record must be kept in case of any incidents. You probably unconsciously carry out a risk assessment whenever you do anything; for example, when crossing the road, you would automatically check the traffic flow before stepping out.

Policies and procedures

You will need to follow your organisation's policies and procedures, which should include:

- access and fair assessment
- appeals and complaints
- confidentiality of information
- copyright and data protection
- equal opportunities
- equality and diversity
- health and safety.

There may be other requirements such as a dress code, acceptable use of ICT equipment or a behaviour code, and regulations such as Control of Substances Hazardous to Health (COSHH) that you will need to follow.

Activity

Identify the policies, procedures and regulations which will relate to your role as an assessor for your particular subject. How will they impact upon your roles and responsibilities?

Boundaries

You will have professional boundaries within which to work. You will need to know what these are at your organisation, and not overstep them. Boundaries are about knowing where your role as an assessor stops. You may have a learner who needs more support than others; you would not be helping them if you did their work for them. You would be better guiding them to where they could find things out for themselves and giving them autonomy in the learning and assessment process. You may have some learners who have personal problems and not feel confident at giving them advice. Knowing whom to refer them to would ensure they receive expert information. Always remain professional, don't get personally involved with your learners and don't bring your own problems or attitudes to a situation.

Extension Activity

Look at your job description; it might be part of your contract of employment. If you don't have a job description, look at Appendices 1, 2 and 3. Describe the functions you will carry out as an assessor to meet these. Find out if your assessment decisions will be sampled by an internal quality assurer and, if so, who this will be and what they will do.

Minimising risks

When planning to assess your learners you need to be aware of potential risks. This applies not only to those regarding the health, safety and welfare of all concerned, but the types of risks that may be involved in your own area of responsibility for your particular subject. You need to minimise risks such as putting unnecessary stress upon learners, over-assessing, under-assessing or being unfair and expecting too much too soon. Some learners might not be ready to be observed for a practical skill, or feel so pressured by target dates for a theory task that they resort to colluding or plagiarising work from others or the internet.

If learners are under pressure, or have any issues or concerns that have not been addressed, they may decide to leave. Being aware of any risks and taking opportunities to discuss any issues your learner might have should help alleviate any concerns.

There are also risks on your part as an assessor, for example, pressure to pass learners quickly due to funding implications, or favouritism and bias towards some learners over others. You might carry out assessments in the work environment and be visiting places with which you are not familiar. You might have to travel early or late in the dark, find locations on foot, take public transport, or drive to locations you do not know. If you are visiting places on your own, you will be classed as a lone worker and your organisation should have a policy for your protection. If you feel uncomfortable or unsafe at any time, you should get in touch with your supervisor. Having a mobile phone is helpful in such situations; if not, note where the nearest public phone is should you need it. You may find it useful to search the internet for the postcode you are visiting. This will give you a street map and pictures of the local area to enable you to visualise where you are going.

If you are assessing in the work environment, you might come across employers who are not supportive of their staff and may put barriers in their way. For example, someone might make it difficult for you to visit at a certain time to carry out a formal assessment. Careful planning and communication with everyone concerned will be necessary.

It could be that if you have close friends or relatives who you are required to assess, you might not be allowed to, or if you do, your decisions would need to be countersigned by another impartial assessor. If the qualification is accredited, the awarding organisation will give you guidance on this.

If you have any concerns regarding risks to yourself, your learners, or your assessment decisions you must discuss these with your manager.

Extension Activity

What risks do you feel you will encounter as an assessor and how will you overcome them? Have you ever been placed in a risky situation? If so, what would you do differently next time?

Types of assessment

Different subjects will require different types of assessment, which can be carried out formally or informally depending upon the requirements. Formal assessments are usually planned and carried out according to the assessment requirements or criteria, whereas informal assessments can occur at any time to check ongoing progress. You may be familiar with some types such as initial (at the beginning), formative (ongoing) and summative (at the end). Initial assessment helps you ascertain information before your learner commences the programme. Formative assessment can happen at any time during the programme and is usually informal as you can devise your own activities. Summative assessment is usually formal and you must follow the requirements of the awarding organisation if the programme is accredited by them.

Assessment types are different from assessment methods. A method is how the assessment type will be used and can be formal or informal. Formal methods count towards the achievement of a qualification whereas informal methods check ongoing progress.

Formal assessment methods include:	Informal assessment methods include:
• assignments • essays • exams • observations • oral and written questions • recognition of prior learning (RPL) • reviewing work products and learner evidence • tests	• discussions • gapped handouts • group work • journals/diaries • peer and self-assessment • puzzles and quizzes • role plays • word searches

Table 1.2: Formal and informal assessment methods

You will use different methods depending upon whether you are assessing knowledge or performance. Knowledge is usually assessed by assignments, essays and tests. Performance is usually assessed by observation, questions and discussions. These will vary depending upon the subject you are assessing. Formal assessment activities are usually provided by the awarding organisation (if you are assessing an accredited qualification). You will be able to devise your own informal methods to check ongoing progress.

All assessment types and methods should be suitable to the level of your learners. A level 1 learner might struggle to maintain a journal of their progress and a level 2 learner may not be mature enough to accept peer feedback. A level 3 learner may feel a puzzle is too easy, and so on. See the Introduction for details of levels. Some learners may respond better to informal assessment rather than formal assessment. You need to consider the assessment requirements for your subject, and how you can best implement these, without changing the assessment criteria.

Example

Maria sees her group of learners once a week for an Art and Design programme. Each week, she commences the session by asking some questions regarding the topics covered in the previous week. This is formative assessment to ensure her learners have understood the topics taught. At the end of term, she will issue a summative assessment in the form of an assignment, which will formally test their skills and knowledge.

You might have all the details of assessment types and methods provided for you; if not, you will need to carefully select these to suit your subject, the situation and your learners. You might decide to assess your learners on a formative basis throughout their time with you, and with a summative test at the end. This would enable you to see how they are progressing, and whether they will be ready or not for the formal test. You might be provided with tests or assignments for your learners to complete at set times during the programme. To be sure your learners are ready you could use activities, quizzes and smaller tasks for them to carry out. This would make the assessment process more interesting and highlight any areas that need further development. If you are assessing a programme whereby the activities are provided for you, for example tests or exams, there is often the tendency to teach purely what is required to achieve a pass. Learners may therefore not gain valuable additional skills and knowledge. Teaching to pass tests does not maximise your learners' ability and potential.

Table 1.3 on pages 33–34 briefly explains assessment terminology and various types of assessment. The ones you use will be based on whether you assess occupational competence in the work environment or vocational skills, knowledge and understanding elsewhere.

Extension Activity

Refer to the types of assessment in Table 1.3 and choose six types that you might use with your learners. Summarise the types of risk that might be involved when using them and explain how you could minimise risks when planning assessments with your learners.

Type	Description
Academic	Assessment of theory or knowledge.
Adaptive	Questions are selected during the test on the basis of their difficulty, in response to an estimate of the learner's ability.
Analytic scoring	A method of scoring grades for tests such as speaking and writing. For example, a writing test would have an analytic score based on grammar and vocabulary.
Aptitude	A diagnostic test to assess a learner's ability for a particular job or vocation.
Assessor led	Assessment is planned and carried out by the assessor, for example, an observation.
Benchmarking	A way of evaluating learner performance against an accepted standard. Once a standard is set, it can be used as a basis for the expectation of achievements with other groups/learners.
Blended	Using more than one assessment method in different locations, for example, observation in the work environment backed up with online assessments.
Competence based	Criteria that learners need to perform in the work environment.
Criterion referencing	Assessing prescribed aspects a learner must achieve to meet a certain standard.
Diagnostic	A specific assessment relating to a particular topic or subject and level, which builds on initial assessment. Sometimes called a *skills test*. The results determine what needs to be learnt or assessed in order to progress further. Some types of diagnostic assessments can also identify learners with dyslexia, dyspraxia, dysgraphia, dyscalculia, etc.
Differentiation	Organising teaching, learning and assessment to suit learners' abilities and needs.
Direct	Evidence provided by a learner towards their qualification, for example, products from their work environment.
Evidence	Assessment is based upon items a learner provides to prove their knowledge and competence.
External	Assessments set and marked externally by an awarding organisation.
Formal	Assessment that involves the recognition and recording of achievement, often leading to certification of an accredited qualification.
Formative	Ongoing, interim or continuous assessment. Can be used to assess skills and/or knowledge in a progressive way, to build on topics learnt and plan future learning and assessments. Often referred to as assessment *for* learning, allowing additional learning to take place prior to further assessments.
Holistic	Assessing several aspects of a qualification, programme or job specification at the same time.
Independent	An aspect of the qualification is assessed by someone who has not been involved with the learner for any other part of their learning or assessment.
Indirect	Evidence provided by others regarding a learner's progress, for example, a witness testimony from their supervisor.
Informal	Assessment that is in addition to formal assessment, for example, questioning during a review of progress with a learner, or an observation during a group activity.
Initial	Assessment at the beginning of a programme or unit, relating to the subject being learnt and assessed, to identify a learner's starting point and level. Initial assessment can also include learning styles tests, and literacy, language, numeracy and ICT tests. The latter can be used as a basis to help and support learners.
Integrated	Information acquired in a learning context is put into practice and assessed in the learner's work environment.

Internal	Assessments carried out within an organisation, either internally set and marked, or externally set by the relevant awarding organisation and internally marked.
Ipsative	A process of self assessment to recognise development. Learners match their own achievements against a set of standards or their own previous achievements. This is useful for learners to consider their progress and development. However, they do need to work autonomously and be honest with themselves.
Learner led	Learners produce evidence and let their assessor know when they are ready to be assessed.
Norm referencing	Comparing the results of learner achievements to each other, for example, setting a pass mark to enable a certain percentage of a group to achieve or not.
Objective	An assessment decision that is based around the criteria being assessed, not a personal opinion or decision.
Predictive	An indication of how well a test predicts future performance in a relevant skill.
Process	The assessment of routine skills or techniques, for example, to ensure a learner is following a set process or procedure.
Process (as in teaching)	Teaching more than is required for the learner to achieve, for example, teaching keyboard skills to a learner who is taking a word-processing qualification (i.e. it's not in the syllabus but it is helpful).
Product	The outcome is assessed, not the process of making it, for example, a painting or a working model.
Product (as in teaching)	Only teaching the minimum amount required to pass an assessment.
Proficiency	An assessment to test ability or skills without reference to any specific programme of learning, for example, riding a bicycle.
Profiling	A way of recording learner achievements for each individual aspect of an assessment. Checklists can be a useful way to evidence these. More than one assessor can be involved in the process.
Psychometric	A test of psychological qualities, for example, intelligence and personality.
Qualitative	Assessment is based upon individual responses to open questions given to learners. Clear criteria must be stated for the assessor to make a decision as questions can be vague or misinterpreted.
Quantitative	Assessment is based upon yes/no or true/false responses, agree/disagree statements or multiple choice tests, giving a clear right or wrong answer. Totals can be added to give results, for example, 8 out of 10. Learners could pass purely by guessing the correct answers.
Screening	A process to determine if a learner has a particular need, for example, in language, literacy or numeracy.
Subjective	A personal decision by the assessor, where the assessment criteria might not be clearly stated. This can be unfair to a learner.
Summative	Assessment at the end of a programme or unit, for example, an exam. If a learner does not pass, they will usually have the opportunity to retake. Often known as assessment *of* learning, as it shows what has been achieved from the learning process.
Triangulation	Using more than one assessment method, for example, observation, oral questioning and a test. This helps ensure the reliability and authenticity of a learner's work and makes the assessment process more interesting.
Vocational	Job-related practical assessment, usually in a learner's work environment.

Table 1.3: Types of assessment

Methods of assessment

Assessment can only take place once learning has occurred, but how do you know that learning has occurred? You might be able to answer this by saying, 'I'll ask questions', or 'I'll see my learner working'. That's fine, if you know what questions to ask and how your learner should respond, or what you expect to see your learner perform. If you don't know this, you will need to plan and use suitable methods to assess your learners when you know they are ready.

To effectively plan how you will assess your learners, you need to use methods which are safe, valid, fair and reliable.

- Safe: e.g. the methods used are ethical, there is little chance of plagiarism, the work can be confirmed as authentic, confidentially is taken into account, learning and assessment is not compromised in any way, nor the learner's experience or potential to achieve (safe in this context does not relate to health and safety but to the methods used).

- Valid: e.g. the methods used are based on the requirements of the qualification, programme or job specification.

- Fair: e.g. the methods used are appropriate to all learners at the required level, taking into account any particular needs.

- Reliable: e.g. a similar decision would be made with similar learners.

Example

If you allow your learners to copy text from the internet to answer questions without quoting their source it will be deemed unsafe. If you set a test which doesn't accurately reflect the assessment criteria, it is invalid. If you give some learners more help than others it is unfair. If you devise a set of questions, and use them with different groups of learners, they may discuss them among themselves, therefore rendering their responses unreliable.

There are several different assessment methods, for example, observations, questioning, tests and exams. If assessment activities are not provided for you, you will need to devise your own methods. Always take into account your learners' needs, their level of achievement and the subject requirements before planning to use any assessment activities. The methods you choose will depend upon what you will assess, where and how. If you are assessing units that are on the Qualifications and Credit Framework (QCF) these are known as *knowledge* units (to assess understanding) and *performance* units (to assess skills). See the Introduction for details regarding the QCF.

Assessment should never be just for the sake of assessing. There should always be a reason for any assessment activity you carry out, the main one being to find out if learning has taken place and whether the learner is ready to progress further.

Never be afraid to try something different, particularly with formative assessments that you can design yourself. You could use puzzles, quizzes or crosswords as a fun and active way of informally assessing your learners' progress. Try searching the internet for free software to help you create these.

Extension Activity

Think about the learners you have at present, or those whom you will be assessing in the future. How do you know that learning has taken place and that they will be ready to be summatively assessed? Look at the following assessment methods in table 1.4, decide which methods you could use for formative and summative purposes, and state the advantages and limitations to their use for your subject.

Table 1.4 on pages 37–45 lists the assessment methods and activities you could use, along with a brief description, their strengths and their limitations. When using any activity, you need to ensure it is inclusive, and differentiate for individual learning styles and needs, learner difficulties and/ or disabilities. Always follow health and safety guidelines, and carry out any relevant risk assessments where applicable. Make sure your learners are aware why they are being assessed, and don't overcomplicate your activities.

Table 1.4: Assessment methods and activities

Method	Description	Strengths	Limitations
Assignments	Several activities or tasks, practical or theoretical, to assess various aspects of a qualification over a period of time.	Consolidates learning. Several aspects of a qualification can be assessed. Some assignments are set by the awarding organisation who will give clear marking criteria.	Everything must have been taught beforehand. Questions can be misinterpreted if written by someone else. Can be time consuming. Must be individually assessed and written feedback given. Assessor might be biased when marking.
Blended assessments	Using more than one method of assessment, usually including technology.	Several methods of assessment can be combined, enabling all learning styles to be reached.	Not all learners may have access to the technology.
Buzz groups	Short topics to be discussed in small groups.	Allows learner interaction and focuses ideas. Checks understanding. Doesn't require formal feedback.	Learners may digress. Specific points could be lost. Checking individual learning has taken place may be difficult.
Case studies/ scenarios	Can be a hypothetical situation, a description of an actual event or an incomplete event, enabling learners to explore the situation.	Can make topics more realistic, enhancing motivation and interest. Can be carried out individually or in a group situation. Builds on current knowledge and experience.	If carried out as a group activity, roles should be defined and individual contributions assessed. Time should be allowed for a debrief. Must have clear outcomes, which can be difficult to define. Can be time consuming to prepare and assess.
Checklists	A list of criteria which must be met to confirm competence or achievement.	Can form part of an ongoing record of achievement or a profile. Assessment can take place when a learner is ready. Ensures all criteria are met and a record maintained.	Learners may lose their copy and not remember what they have achieved.

Method	Description	Strengths	Limitations
Discussions with learners (also known as a professional discussion)	A conversation between the assessor and learner based around the assessment criteria.	Ideal way to assess aspects which are more difficult to observe, are rare occurrences, or take place in restricted or confidential settings. Useful to support observations to check knowledge. Learners can describe how they carry out various activities.	A record must be kept of the discussion, for example, audio/digital/visual, along with notes. Needs careful planning as it's a discussion not a question and answer session. Learners need time to prepare. Assessor needs to be experienced at questioning and listening skills. Assessor needs to be experienced at using open and probing questions, and listening carefully to the responses.
Discussions/ debates	Learners talk about a relevant topic that contributes to the assessment criteria.	All learners can participate. Allows freedom of viewpoints, questions and discussions.	Easy to digress. Assessor needs to keep the group focused and set a time limit. Some learners may not get involved, others may take over – assessor needs to manage the contributions of individuals. Can be time consuming. Learners may need to research a topic in advance. Can lead to arguments.
E-assessments/ online assessments	*Electronic assessment* – assessment using information and communication technology (ICT). *Synchronous* – assessor and learner are simultaneously present, communicating in real time. *Asynchronous* – assessor and learner are interacting at different times.	Teaching, learning and assessment can take place in a virtual learning environment (VLE). Assessment can take place at a time to suit learners. Participation is widened. Results and feedback can be instantly generated. Ensures reliability. Less paperwork for the assessor. Improves ICT skills. Can be blended with other assessment methods. Groups, blogs, forums and chat rooms can be set up to improve communication.	Learners need access to a computer and need to be computer literate. Self discipline is needed, along with clear targets. Authenticity of learner's work may need validating. Technical support may be required. Reliable internet connection needed.

Method	Description	Strengths	Limitations
Essays	A formal piece of written text, produced by a learner, for a specific topic.	Useful for academic subjects. Can check a learner's language and literacy skills at specific levels.	Not suitable for lower level learners. Marking can be time consuming. Plagiarism can be an issue. Doesn't usually have a right or wrong answer therefore difficult to grade. Learners need good writing skills.
Examinations	A formal test that should be carried out in certain conditions.	Can be open book, or open notes, enabling learners to have books and notes with them. Some learners like the challenge of a formal examination and cope well.	Invigilation required. Security arrangements to be in place prior to, and afterwards for papers. Learners may have been taught purely to pass expected questions by using past papers, therefore they may forget everything afterwards. Some learners may be anxious.
Group work	Enables learners to carry out a specific activity, for example, problem solving. Can be practical or theoretical.	Allows interaction between learners. Encourages participation and variety. Rotating group members enables all learners to work with each other.	Careful management by the assessor is required regarding time limits, progress, and ensuring all group members are clear about the requirements. Could be personality problems with team members or large groups. One person may dominate. Difficult to assess individual contributions. Time is needed for a thorough debrief and feedback.
Holistic	Enables learners to demonstrate several aspects of a programme or qualification at the same time.	Holistic assessment of a performance unit could incorporate aspects of a knowledge unit. Similar criteria from different units can be assessed at the same time. Makes evidence collection and demonstration of competence much more efficient.	Could confuse the learner if aspects were assessed which were not planned for.

Method	Description	Strengths	Limitations
Homework	Activities carried out between sessions, for example, answering questions, to check knowledge.	Learners can complete at a time and place that suits them. Maintains interest between sessions. Encourages learners to stretch themselves further. Consolidates learning so far.	Clear time limits must be set. Learners might not do it, or get someone else to do it for them. Must be marked/assessed and individual feedback given.
Icebreakers/ teambuilding exercises	A fun and light-hearted way of introducing learners and topics.	A good way of learners getting to know each other, and for the assessor to observe skills and attitudes. Can revitalise a flagging session.	Not all learners may want to take part. Some learners may see these as insignificant – careful explanations are needed to link the experience to the topic.
Interviews	A one-to-one discussion, usually before a learner commences a programme, or part way through to discuss progress.	Enables the assessor to see how much a learner knows. Enables the assessor to get to know each learner, and discuss any issues.	Not all learners may react well when interviewed. Needs careful planning, and consistency of questions between learners.
Learner statements	Learners write how they have met the assessment criteria.	Enables learners to take ownership of their achievements.	Learners might misinterpret the assessment criteria and/or write too much or too little. An additional assessment method should be used to confirm competence.
Learning journal/ diary	Learners keep a record of their progress, their reflections and thoughts, and reference these to the assessment criteria.	Helps assess language and literacy skills. Useful for higher level programmes.	Should be specific to the learning taking place and be analytical rather than descriptive. Contents need to remain confidential. Can be time consuming and/or difficult to read.

Method	Description	Strengths	Limitations
Observations	Watching learners perform a skill.	Enables skills to be seen in action. Learners can make a mistake (if it is safe) enabling them to realise their errors. Can assess several aspects of a qualification at the same time (holistic assessment).	Timing must be arranged to suit each learner. Communication needs to take place with others (if applicable). No permanent record unless visually recorded. Questions must be asked to confirm understanding. Assessor might not be objective with decision. Learner might put on an act for the assessor which isn't how they normally perform.
Peer assessments	Learners giving feedback to their peers after an activity.	Promotes learner and peer interaction and involvement. Learners may accept comments from peers better than those from the assessor. Enables learners to assess each other. Activities can often correct misunderstandings and consolidate learning without intervention by the assessor.	Everyone needs to understand the assessment criteria and requirements. Needs to be carefully managed to ensure no personality conflicts or unjustified comments. Assessor needs to confirm progress and achievements as it might be different. Some peers may be anxious about giving feedback. Should be supported with other assessment methods. Needs careful management and training in how to give feedback.
Portfolios of evidence	A formal record of evidence (manual or electronic) produced by learners, towards a qualification.	Ideal for learners who don't like formal exams. Can be compiled over a period of time. Learner centred; promotes autonomy. Evidence can be left in its natural location and viewed by the assessor.	Authenticity and currency to be checked. Computer access required to assess electronic portfolios. Tendency for learners to produce a large quantity of evidence. All evidence must be cross-referenced. Can be time consuming to assess. Confidentiality of documents within the portfolio must be maintained.

Method	Description	Strengths	Limitations
Practical activities/ tasks	Assesses a learner's skills in action.	Actively involves learners. Can meet all learning styles if carefully set.	Some learners may not respond well to practical activities. Can be time consuming to create.
Presentations	Learners deliver a topic, often using audio-visual aids.	Can be individual or in a group. Can assess skills, knowledge and attitudes.	If a group presentation, individual contributions must be assessed. Some learners may be nervous or anxious. Practice sessions are useful, but time consuming.
Products	Evidence produced by a learner to prove competence, for example, paintings, models, video, audio, photos, documents.	Assessor can see the final outcome. Learners feel a sense of achievement, for example, by displaying their work in an exhibition.	Authenticity needs to be checked if the work in progress has not been seen.
Projects	A longer term activity enabling learners to provide evidence which meets the assessment criteria.	Can be interesting and motivating. Can be individual or group led. Can meet all learning styles. Encourages research skills. Learners could choose their own topics and devise tasks.	Clear outcomes must be set, along with a time limit; must be relevant, realistic and achievable. Progress should be checked regularly. If a group is carrying out the project, ensure each individual's input is assessed. Assessor might be biased when marking. Thorough feedback should be given.
Puzzles, quizzes, word searches, crosswords, etc.	A fun way of assessing learning in an informal way.	Fun activities to test knowledge, skills and/or attitudes. Useful back-up activity if learners finish an activity earlier than planned. Useful way to assess progress of lower level learners. Good for assessing retention of facts.	Can seem trivial to mature learners. Does not assess a learner's level of understanding or ability to apply their knowledge to situations. Can be time consuming to create and assess.

Method	Description	Strengths	Limitations
Questions	A key technique for assessing understanding and stimulating thinking, can be formal or informal. Questions can be closed, hypothetical, leading, open, probing, multiple choice, etc.	Can be multiple choice, short answer or long essay style. Can challenge and promote a learner's potential. A question bank can be devised, which could be used again and again for all learners. Can test critical arguments or thinking and reasoning skills. Oral questions suit some learners more than others, e.g. a learner with dyslexia might prefer to talk through their responses.	Closed questions only give a yes or no response, which doesn't demonstrate knowledge. Questions must be written carefully, i.e. be unambiguous, and can be time consuming to prepare. If the same questions are used with other learners, they could share their answers. Written responses might be the work of others, i.e. copied or plagiarised. Expected responses or grading criteria need to be produced beforehand to ensure consistency and validity of marking. May need to rephrase some questions if learners are struggling with an answer.
Recognition of prior learning (RPL)	Assessing what has previously taken place to find a suitable starting point for further assessments, equivalent units or exemption units.	Ideal for learners who have achieved aspects of the programme prior to commencement. No need for learners to duplicate work, or be reassessed. Values previous achievements.	Checking the authenticity and currency of the evidence provided is crucial. Can be time consuming for both learner to prove, and the assessor to assess.
Reports, research and dissertations	Learners produce a document to inform, recommend and/or make suggestions based on the assessment criteria.	Useful for higher level learners. Encourages the use of research techniques.	Learners need research and academic writing skills. Time consuming to mark. Plagiarism and authenticity can be an issue.
Role plays	Learners act out a hypothetical situation.	Enables the assessor to observe learners' behaviour. Encourages participation. Can lead to debates. Links theory to practice.	Can be time consuming Clear roles must be defined. Not all learners may want, or be able to, participate. Some learners may get too dramatic. Individual contributions must be assessed. Time needed for a thorough debrief.

Method	Description	Strengths	Limitations
Self-assessment	Learners decide how they have met the assessment criteria, or are progressing at a given time.	Promotes learner involvement and personal autonomy. Encourages learners to check their own work before handing in. Encourages reflection. Learners need to be specific about what they have achieved and what they need to do to complete any gaps.	Learners may feel they are doing better or worse than they actually are. Assessor needs to discuss progress and achievements with each learner to confirm their decisions. Learners need to be specific about what they have achieved and what they need to do to complete any gaps. Difficult to be objective when making a decision.
Skills tests	Designed to find out the level of skill or previous experience/knowledge for a particular subject or vocation.	Could be online or computer based to enable a quick assessment, for example, literacy. Results can be used as starting point for learning or progression.	Learners might be apprehensive of formal tests. Feedback might not be immediate.
Simulation	Imitation or acting out of an event or situation.	Useful when it is not possible to carry out a task for real, for example, to assess whether learners can successfully evacuate a building in a fire.	Only enables an assessment of a hypothetical situation; learners may act very differently in a real situation. Not usually accepted as NVQ evidence.
Tests	A formal assessment situation.	Cost-effective method as the same test can be used with large numbers of learners. Some test responses can be scanned into a computer for marking and analysis. Other tests can be taken at a computer or online and give immediate results.	Needs to be carried out in supervised conditions or via a secure website. Time limits usually required. Can be stressful to learners. Does not take into account any formative progress. Feedback might not be immediate. Learners in other groups might find out the content of the tests from others. Identity of learners needs confirming. If set by an awarding organisation, ensure all aspects of the syllabus have been taught beforehand.

Method	Description	Strengths	Limitations
Tutorials	A one-to-one or group discussion between the assessor and learner, with an agreed purpose, for example, assessing progress so far.	A good way of informally assessing all learners' progress and/or giving feedback. An opportunity for learners to discuss issues or for informal tuition to take place.	Needs to be in a comfortable, safe and quiet environment as confidential issues may be discussed. Time: may overrun. Records should be maintained and action points followed up.
Video/audio	Recorded evidence of actual achievements.	Direct proof of what was achieved by a learner. Can be reviewed by the assessor and internal quality assurer after the event.	Can prove expensive to purchase equipment and storage media. Can be time consuming. Technical support may be required. Storage facilities are required.
Walk and talk	A spoken and visual way of assessing a learner's competence	Enables a learner to walk and talk through their product evidence within their work environment. Gives an audit trail of the evidence relating to the assessment criteria. Saves time producing a full portfolio of evidence; the walk and talk can be recorded as evidence of the discussion. Useful where sensitive and confidential information is dealt with.	A time consuming way of assessing the criteria. Difficult for quality assurers to sample the evidence.
Witness testimonies	A statement from a person who is familiar with the learner (they could also be an expert in the standards being assessed and the occupation of the learner in the work environment).	The witness can confirm competence or achievements for situations which might not regularly occur, or when the assessor cannot be present.	The assessor must confirm the suitability of the witness and check the authenticity of any statements. Learners might write the statement and the witness might sign it, not understanding the content.
Worksheets and gapped handouts	Interactive handouts to check knowledge (can also be electronic). Blank spaces can be used for learners to fill in the missing words.	Informal assessment activity which can be done individually, in pairs or groups. Useful for lower level learners. Can be created at different degrees of difficulty to address differentiation.	Mature learners may consider them inappropriate. Too many worksheets can be boring; learners might not be challenged enough.

Summary

In this chapter you have learnt about:

- key concepts and principles of assessment
- the roles and responsibilities of an assessor
- minimising risks
- types of assessment
- methods of assessment.

Evidence from the completed activities, plus the following, could be used towards the *Principles and practices of assessment* unit, for example:

- written statements cross-referenced to the TAQA unit's assessment criteria
- answers to questions/assignments issued by the awarding organisation
- records of discussions with your assessor.

Cross-referencing grid

This chapter contributes towards the following three TAQA units' assessment criteria. Full details of the learning outcomes and assessment criteria for each TAQA unit can be found in the Appendices.

TAQA unit	Assessment criteria
Understanding the principles and practices of assessment	1.1, 1.2, 1.3, 1.4 2.1 3.4, 3.5 4.1, 4.4 5.1, 5.2 6.1, 6.2 7.1 8.1, 8.3
Assess occupational competence in the work environment	1.1 2.1 4.1, 4.2
Assess vocational skills, knowledge and understanding	1.1 4.1, 4.2

Theory focus

References and further information

Bonnerjea, L (2009) *Safeguarding Adults: Report on the consultation on the review of 'No Secrets'*. London: Department of Health.

Department for Education and Skills (DfES) (2006) *Safeguarding Children and Safer Recruitment in Education*. London: DfES.

Ecclestone, K (2005) *Understanding Assessment and Qualifications in Post-Compulsory Education and Training* (2nd edition). Ashford: NIACE.

Gardner, J (2006) *Assessment and Learning*. London: Sage Publications.

Gravells, A and Simpson, S (2012) *Equality and Diversity in the Lifelong Learning Sector*. Exeter: Learning Matters.

Tummons, J (2011) *Assessing Learning in the Lifelong Learning Sector* (3rd edition). Exeter: Learning Matters.

Websites

Chartered Institute for Educational Assessors: www.ciea.org.uk

COSHH: www.hse.gov.uk/coshh

Disability and the Equality Act: http://tinyurl.com/2vzd5j

Equality and Human Rights Commission: www.equalityhumanrights.com

Fleming's learning styles: www.vark-learn.com

Health and Safety Executive: www.hse.gov.uk

Health and Safety resources: www.hse.gov.uk/services/education/information.htm

Initial assessment tools: www.excellencegateway.org.uk/toolslibrary

Office safety and risk assessments: www.officesafety.co.uk

Ofsted: www.ofsted.gov.uk

Literacy and numeracy online tests: www.move-on.org.uk

CHAPTER 2
ASSESSING
OCCUPATIONAL
COMPETENCE IN THE
WORK ENVIRONMENT

Introduction

In this chapter you will learn about:

- assessment planning in the work environment

- making assessment decisions

- providing feedback to learners and others

- standardising practice

- record keeping – assessment

There are activities and examples which will help you reflect on the above and will assist your knowledge of assessing occupational competence in the work environment. Completing the activities will help you to gather evidence towards the TAQA *Assessing occupational competence in the work environment* unit. At the end of each section is an extension activity to stretch and challenge your learning further.

At the end of the chapter is a list of possible evidence which could be used towards the TAQA *Assessing occupational competence in the work environment* unit.

A cross-referencing grid shows how the content of this chapter contributes towards the three TAQA units' assessment criteria. There is also a theory focus with relevant references, further information and websites to which you might like to refer.

Assessment planning in the work environment

Assessing learners or employees in the work environment will help you confirm their competence towards a qualification or their job role. Before you commence the planning process, you need to be fully conversant with what you are going to assess, where this will be, and any requirements and regulations for your particular subject.

If you are assessing towards a qualification which is accredited through an awarding organisation, a certificate will be issued upon successful completion. The awarding organisation will monitor the delivery, assessment and quality assurance of the qualification to ensure all their guidelines are being followed. If you have not already done so, you will need to obtain a copy of the qualification handbook which will contain all the details regarding the assessment requirements.

If you are assessing an employee's competence towards their job role or a new skill they are putting into practice, this is known as *non-accredited* as a certificate will not be issued by an awarding organisation. However, a *record of achievement* might be given to the employee once they have proved their competence. This could be issued by their employer, or the organisation for which you are assessing. For the purpose of this chapter, the term *learner* will be used for both learners and employees.

Vocational qualifications are an excellent way for competent employees to demonstrate their skills and knowledge in their work environment and gain a qualification. However, if there are aspects of the qualification with which they are not familiar, training will need to take place. An initial assessment of skills and knowledge would greatly help identify what may need to be learnt first, before any further assessment takes place. If you are not familiar with how to teach or train, there are relevant qualifications you can take such as the Award in Preparing to Teach in the Lifelong Learning Sector (PTLLS), which is the first step in the teacher training process.

When assessing learners in their place of work, it is best to plan ahead to arrange your visits according to location, for example, assessing learners in close proximity to ease the time and cost spent travelling. Out of courtesy, notify your learner's employer in advance, in case there is any reason they cannot accommodate you on a particular day. You will also need to check travel, transport and/or parking arrangements.

Activity

When you are planning to assess in the work environment, can you use public transport, or is there a company vehicle you can use? If you use your own vehicle, find out how you can reclaim any expenses. Are there any protocols you need to follow when visiting other organisations? If you are not sure, find out, as you may need to confirm dates and times, and carry appropriate identification.

If your learner works shifts or during the weekend, you will need to visit when they are working, as it isn't fair to ask them to change their work patterns just to suit you. If for any reason an assessment is cancelled, make sure a revised date is scheduled as soon as possible and inform all concerned. Always confirm your visit one or two days beforehand just in case there is any reason you cannot go.

If you are currently working towards an assessment qualification yourself, you may need to have all your decisions and records countersigned by another assessor who is qualified in your subject area. This could be your supervisor or mentor, who might also observe your practice to have confidence in your role as an assessor.

Initial assessment

You will need to ascertain information about your learners to help them progress towards an achievable aim. Everyone is different and the starting point for each learner will differ depending upon their prior knowledge and skills, and any particular needs they may have. This will help you decide whether they can be assessed straight away, or if they need training or practice in their work environment. They might have recently gained new knowledge and need time to put theory into practice, or they might have achieved something already which can be taken into account – known as recognition of prior learning (RPL). Initial assessment is the first stage of the assessment cycle (see Figure 1.1 on page 15) and will help you ascertain these details and more. It can be carried out by a discussion with your learner, completion of a form (manual or online), or an interview. It will also help you obtain further information to help your learners, for example, any specific assessment requirements they may have, their learning style, the language for assessment (e.g. Welsh or bilingual) or any further training and support they may need.

Diagnostic assessments can be part of initial assessment and are a specific way of finding out about a learner's current skills in a particular subject. They can also be used to identify learners with dyslexia, or whether learners need support with language and literacy. The results can lead to additional training and support while your learner is working towards their aim.

Example

Sharron has completed an initial assessment process which was designed to assess her knowledge and skills towards the level 2 Diploma in Travel and Tourism. Sharron had started the qualification at another organisation prior to moving to the area. Her current assessor was able to see her evidence for three units which she had completed fairly recently. Sharron was therefore accredited with these units once her assessor had confirmed all the requirements had been met. She therefore did not need to be reassessed for these units. The initial assessment process also incorporated a skills scan to obtain information regarding Sharron's level of language, literacy, numeracy and ICT.

It could be that your learner has achieved some units of a qualification elsewhere and might just need to provide their certificate as evidence of prior achievement. If the achieved units are listed on the Qualifications and Credit Framework (QCF), they should automatically be recognised and classed as an exemption.

Initial assessment will help you to:

- agree an appropriate assessment plan, with suitable targets and dates
- allow for differentiation and meeting individual requirements
- ensure learners are taking the right programme at the right level
- identify an appropriate starting point for each learner
- identify any information which needs to be shared with colleagues
- identify any specific additional support needs
- identify previous experience and achievements
- identify learning styles
- identify specific requirements, for example, language, literacy, numeracy and ICT

- inspire and motivate learners

- involve learners, giving them confidence to agree and achieve their targets.

Activity

Find out what initial and diagnostic assessments are used at your organisation. Will it be your responsibility to administer these, or is there a specialist to do this? If possible, carry out an initial assessment with a learner. How will you use the results to help plan what your learner will do and when?

Once you have the information you need from the initial assessment process, you can agree an assessment plan with your learner. If you are not familiar with initial assessment documents, there are lots of materials available online. If you get the opportunity, carry out a search for *initial assessment* via the internet.

The template in Table 2.1 opposite is a form which could be used for initial assessment purposes.

Assessment planning

Once you have the results from initial assessments, you can begin the assessment planning process. An assessment plan is a formal agreement between you and your learner of what will be assessed, how and when.

The assessment requirements will be written in a specific way, for example:

- ability outcomes

- aims and objectives

- assessment criteria

- evidence requirements

- learning outcomes

- performance criteria

- standards

- statements of competence.

Example

Initial assessment		
Name: Date: Programme/qualification/job specification: Venue:		
What relevant experience do you have?		
What relevant qualifications do you have? *If you have achieved any units on the Qualifications and Credit Framework (QCF), please state them here.*		
Have you completed a learning styles questionnaire? If YES, what is your preferred style of learning? If NO, please complete the questionnaire at www.vark-learn.com and note your results here:	YES/NO Learning style results: V: A: R: K:	
Do you have any particular learning needs or special requirements? If YES, please state here, or talk to your assessor in confidence.	YES/NO	
Are you confident at using a computer? If YES, what experience or qualifications do you have?	YES/NO	Skills Scan Results: ICT:
Would you like help with written/spoken English and literacy?	YES/NO	Skills Scan Results: Language and literacy:
Would you like help with numeracy?	YES/NO	Skills Scan Results: Numeracy:
Why have you decided to take this programme/ qualification? *(continue overleaf)*		
An individual assessment plan should now be agreed. Signed assessor: Signed learner:		

Table 2.1: Initial assessment template

All qualifications on the QCF will use the terms *learning outcomes* and *assessment criteria*. The learning outcomes state what the learner *will do*, and the assessment criteria state what the learner *can do*.

Units are either *knowledge based* (to assess understanding) or *performance based* (to assess competence). Usually, the knowledge units will state what the learner *will do* in sentences beginning with *understand*. What the learner *can do* is stated in sentences beginning with verbs such as *explain*.

The performance units use learning outcomes such as *be able to* and assessment criteria such as *demonstrate*. This helps differentiate between theory and practice. However, there are some units which combine knowledge and performance into one unit if the qualification is small, for example, an Award. See the Introduction for further information regarding the QCF.

Activity

Look at Appendices 1 and 2 at the back of this book. You will see that Appendix 1 is a knowledge unit and Appendix 2 is a performance unit. You can tell this by the different verbs used for the learning outcomes and assessment criteria. If you are working towards these units yourself, you will probably complete an assignment for the knowledge unit and be observed for the performance unit. If so, speak to your assessor and find out how you will be assessed and when.

The methods you use to assess your learners will depend upon whether you are assessing knowledge or performance. The most commonly used methods for assessing performance in the work environment are:

- observations
- examining work products produced by your learner
- asking questions – written or oral
- holding discussions with your learner
- obtaining witness testimonies, for example, from a supervisor
- reading your learner's written statements
- recognising your learner's prior learning (RPL).

If you are assessing a qualification, these methods should be stated for you. If not, you will need to decide on what is most appropriate. Assessment should be a two-way process between you and your learner; you need to plan what you are going to do, and they need to know what is expected of them and when. It could be that you will assess units or aspects in a different order to those stated. For example, instead of assessing Unit 1 before any others, you might decide with your learner that Unit 3 could be assessed first as they are already performing the requirements which are included in that unit.

The way you plan to assess your learners will depend upon the:

- assessment type and method
- assessment strategy from the awarding organisation (if applicable)
- dates, times and duration of assessment activities
- individual learner and qualification/employment level
- location and environment
- organisational budget
- requirements for making decisions and giving feedback
- resources and materials available
- special requirements or particular learner needs
- staff availability and expertise
- subject or qualification, i.e. workplace competence or a vocational qualification
- type of evidence required.

The planning process should involve a discussion between you and your learner, with the chance to set realistic dates and targets. However, it could be that when you do assess your learner, they are not quite as ready as anticipated.

Example

Joan is assessing the level 2 Award in Floristry. She visits each learner once a month in their place of work to observe their competence and asks questions to check their knowledge. While carrying out an assessment with Ben, she realises he is not quite competent in the area she had planned to assess. Joan demonstrates how to perform one of the tasks expected and then Ben attempts it on his own. Joan asks Ben to practise this over the next few days and arranges to return the following month to carry out a formal assessment.

In this example, Joan has carried out an impromptu training session with Ben by demonstrating the task. She then encouraged him to do it himself while she was still present, and then on his own afterwards. Joan could assess other aspects of the qualification while she is there if Ben feels confident. In this way, the visit can lead to an achievement and the assessment plan can be updated as necessary. You will need to be patient with your learners as it takes time to consolidate learning and put theory into practice.

If you are demonstrating something in front of a group of learners, always check if they are left- or right-handed as this could change the way they view things. When they look at you, your right hand will be on their left. If you are demonstrating on a one-to-one basis, try to stand or sit next to your learner rather than facing them.

Assessment planning should be specific, measurable, achievable, realistic and time bound (SMART).

- **S**pecific – the activity relates only to what is being assessed and is clearly stated.
- **M**easurable – the activity can be measured against the assessment requirements, allowing any gaps to be identified.
- **A**chievable – the activity can be achieved at the right level.
- **R**ealistic – the activity is relevant and will give consistent results.
- **T**ime bound – target dates and times can be agreed.

Planning SMART assessment activities will ensure all the assessment requirements will be met by your learners, providing they have acquired the necessary skills and knowledge beforehand.

Assessment planning should provide opportunities for both you and your learners to obtain and use information regarding progress and achievement. It should also be flexible in order to respond to any emerging ideas and skills, for example the use of new technology. The way you plan should include strategies to ensure that your learners understand what they are working towards and the criteria that will be assessed. You should also plan how and when you will give feedback. It could be verbally immediately after the assessment, the next time you see your learner, or by e-mail or other written means. However, the sooner the better, whilst everything is fresh for both of you.

You may be able to observe naturally occurring situations in addition to what had originally been planned. Learners might be able to demonstrate several aspects from different units at the same time, known as *holistic* assessment. Rather than planning to assess individual units on different occasions, you could discuss your learner's job role with them to identify which assessment criteria from other units could be demonstrated at the same time. While the assessment might take longer, it would reduce the number of visits and therefore the inconvenience to all involved. Your learner would need to be ready to demonstrate their competence, therefore don't plan to assess unless they are ready. Never arrange to assess your learner if they are not ready, as this could demoralise them and waste time. Holistic assessment should make evidence collection and demonstration of competence much more efficient.

Example

Rafael is due to assess Sheila for the Level 3 Certificate in Assessing Vocational Achievement, which consists of the following three units.

1. Understanding the principles and practice of assessment.

2. Assess occupational competence in the work environment.

3. Assess vocational skills, knowledge and understanding.

Units 2 and 3 have almost identical assessment criteria for learning outcomes 3 and 4. Rafael is therefore able to plan to assess these all at the same time, providing Sheila can provide the required evidence.

Holistic assessment is beneficial to all concerned when assessing occupational competence, particularly in a work environment. It could be that you carry out a holistic assessment and find your learner is competent at most but not all of the criteria you planned to assess. If this is the case, you can still sign off what they have achieved and then update the assessment plan to assess the remaining criteria on another occasion. Alternatively, you might be able to ask questions or hold a discussion with your learner to evidence the gaps, if this is acceptable. If so, you would need to keep of record of what was asked, perhaps using a *Performance and knowledge report*, an example of which can be found in Chapter 3.

You could also involve witnesses: these are other people the learner is in contact with who could give a statement or testimony as to their competence, for example, their supervisor. They will write how your learner has met the requirements; however, you will need to liaise with them to confirm the authenticity of their statements. If witnesses are involved, they will need to be briefed as to what they are expected to do, and they must be familiar with the subject being assessed. You might also need to check a copy of the witness's certificates and curriculum vitae.

Always ask your learners if there is anything you can do to help make their assessment experience a positive one. For example, ensure you face your learners when speaking to assist anyone hard of hearing, or give them written questions instead of asking oral questions. If you use printed handouts make sure they are in a font, size and colour to suit any particular learner requirements.

Assessment planning should be short term and long term, to allow formative and summative assessment to take place. Including your learners in the planning process will help identify what they have learnt, how and when they will be assessed, and allow for communication to take place to clarify any points or concerns.

When planning to assess, you should have a rationale, i.e. to consider who, what, when, where, why and how (WWWWWH) assessment will take place. This information should always be agreed with your learners beforehand. If you are assessing on an individual basis, the assessment planning process should be formalised, and an assessment plan completed and agreed. When the assessment has taken place or when you review your learner's progress, the plan can be updated.

Careful assessment planning and prior knowledge of your learner's previous achievements are the key to ensuring everyone involved understands what will take place and when.

The example in Table 2.2 opposite is an *assessment plan and review* record.

The assessment plan is like a written contract between you and your learner, towards the achievement of their qualification or job role. It can be reviewed, amended and updated at any time.

Informal assessments will not require an assessment plan, for example, peer feedback, puzzles and quizzes if they are just to check ongoing learning. However, you must always be SMART when using any assessment activities to ensure they have a purpose.

Assessment planning is a crucial part of the teaching and learning process. If it is not carried out correctly and comprehensively, problems may occur

Example

Assessment plan and review record					
Learner: Irene Jones			Assessor: Jenny Smith		
Qualification: Level 1 Certificate in Hospitality & Catering			Registration number: 1234ABCD		
Date commenced: 6 January 2012			Expected completion date: 17 December 2012		
Date	Aspects to be assessed	Date achieved	Assessment details Planning – methods of assessment, activities and SMART targets Review – revisions to plan, achievements and issues discussed	Target/ review date	Agreed by (assessor and learner to sign) (countersigned if necessary by another assessor)
10 Jan	Unit 101 Maintenance of a safe, hygienic and secure working environment		Planning – an observation will take place on 6 February at the County Leisure Centre to assess competence in the workplace for unit 101. The awarding organisation's checklists will be used for this purpose. An observation will take place, oral questions will be asked and a discussion will take place based on the knowledge requirements. A witness testimony will be obtained from Irene's supervisor. Irene has a copy of the assessment criteria and we have discussed the requirements of the following learning outcomes of unit 101 today: 1. Be able to maintain personal health and hygiene. 2. Know how to maintain personal health and hygiene. 3. Be able to help maintain a hygienic, safe and secure workplace. 4. Know how to maintain a hygienic, safe and secure workplace.	Target: 6 February 2012 Review: 6 April 2012	*J Smith* *I Jones*

Table 2.2: Assessment plan and review record

which could disadvantage your learners and prevent them from being successful. When planning assessments, you will need to take into account equality of opportunity, inclusivity and differentiation within the assessment process. Never assume everything is fine just because your learners don't complain. Always include your learners in the assessment planning and review process in case there is something you don't know that you need to act upon.

Extension Activity

Consider the WWWWWH of the assessment planning process for your particular subject and, if possible, agree an assessment plan with a learner. Ensure you are familiar with the assessment criteria you will be assessing against. Who else will you need to involve when creating the assessment plan (besides your learner), what will you assess, when, where, why and how will you do it?

Making assessment decisions

To know that learning has occurred, some form of assessment must take place resulting in a decision. All decisions should be in accordance with the assessment requirements and full records must be maintained, usually for at least three years. It is quite a responsibility to confirm an achievement (or otherwise) as it can affect your learner's personal and professional development. Your learner may need to pass certain criteria to achieve a promotion at work, or they may want to achieve a qualification for personal fulfilment. To make a decision as to whether your learner has achieved, you need to ensure all the required assessment requirements have been met. You also need to be confident yourself that you understand what you are assessing. When assessing, you must always remain *objective*, i.e. by making a decision based on your learner's competence towards set criteria. You should not be *subjective*, i.e. by making a decision based on your own opinions or other factors such as the learner's personality. However, some qualifications or job roles might require the learner to have the correct attitude and manners as part of their job role.

You might observe your learner's skills and then ask questions to check their understanding. Don't be tempted to give them a grade, for example, a distinction or a merit; they have either met or not met the requirements. If your learner did not perform according to the requirements, or answered questions incorrectly, then they will need to redo it. You might need to rephrase your instructions or questions. It could be that your learner does know the correct response, but your question was vague or ambiguous.

Any written work your learners carry out must always be their own and they may have to sign an authentication statement or declaration form. If you have several learners all working towards the same outcomes, you will need to ensure they have not colluded on any formal assessment activities. Otherwise, you might be accrediting them with something their colleagues have done, or even something they have copied from someone else or the internet.

Activity

Ask a colleague if you can observe an assessment activity they are due to carry out. Look at their assessment plan and the materials they use. Observe how they communicate with their learner and others, how they reach their decisions, give feedback and complete their records.

Seeing how other assessors plan and assess will help you develop your own skills.

Your decisions should always be valid, authentic, current, sufficient and reliable (VACSR) – see Chapter 1 for further details. You should also be fair and ethical when assessing your learners and making a judgement.

- Fair – the assessment type was appropriate to all learners at the required level, is inclusive, i.e. available to all, and differentiates for any particular needs.

- Ethical – the assessment took into account confidentiality, integrity, safety, security and learner welfare.

You may find, when assessing, that your learners haven't achieved everything they should have. When making a decision, you need to base this on all the information or evidence available to you at the time. If your learner has not met all the requirements, you need to give constructive feedback, discuss any inconsistencies or gaps and give advice on what they should do next. If your learner disagrees with the assessment process or your decision, they are entitled to follow your organisation's appeals procedure.

If you are having difficulty making a decision, discuss this with your line manager or another assessor to obtain a second opinion. You need to be fully confident when making a decision that what you have assessed meets the relevant criteria. You are not doing your learners any favours by saying they have achieved something when they haven't. You might also notice skills your learners have that they can use in other situations. It is useful to point out any such transferable skills to help them realise other contexts in which they could work. You might also see other aspects demonstrated in addition to those planned. If this is the case, make sure you include them in your decision.

If you are assessing a large amount of work from each learner, it would be a good idea to have a system of signing this in and out. Your learner will have put a lot of effort into their work, and would like to know that you will take reasonable care with it. When you have made your decision and given feedback, you could ask your learner to sign that they have received it back. If your learner was to lose their work, you should have your original assessment records to prove that assessment has taken place.

Recognition of Prior Learning (RPL)

If could be that you have a learner who has achieved an aspect of a qualification or programme elsewhere. Depending upon the evidence they can produce in support of it, they might not have to repeat some or all the requirements. You would need to compare what they have achieved already against the assessment requirements. You can then agree an assessment plan of how to fill the gaps, for example, by a discussion or an observation.

There are occasions where a learner can be exempt altogether, particularly if they are taking a qualification which is on the QCF and they have been accredited with some units already. This is known as an *exemption*.

Example

Robert had achieved the Equality and Diversity unit as part of the Certificate in Teaching in the Lifelong Learning Sector (CTLLS). His job role changed the following year and he was required to take the Diploma in Teaching in the Lifelong Learning Sector (DTLLS). As the Equality and Diversity unit was also in the DTLLS qualification, he was exempt from retaking it.

There will also be occasions where a learner will have an *equivalent* qualification. This means a qualification which was on the previous National Qualifications Framework (NQF) and is similar to a qualification on the current Qualifications and Credit Framework (QCF). For example, the Certificate in Delivering Learning (City & Guilds 7302) is equivalent to the Award in Preparing to Teach in the Lifelong Learning Sector. There is therefore no need for a learner to take the new version. Your learner will have a certificate to prove their achievement; however, you should always check the authenticity of certificates. Details of qualifications and units achieved on the QCF will be held centrally and your learner will be able to show you this via their electronic learner record if necessary.

Factors which could influence your judgement and decision

When making a judgement or decision regarding your learner's achievement, you must always follow the assessment requirements, as well as your organisation's quality assurance measures. You must always remain objective and not let any factors influence your decision if they are not relevant to the subject being assessed. If you are influenced for any reason, then there is a strong risk your learner will not achieve based on their own merit.

The following are factors to consider when making a decision.

- Appeals – if a learner has made an appeal about a decision you have made, you should not feel you must pass them for other assessments if they have not met the requirements. Make sure you follow your organisation's procedures and keep records of your decisions.

- Complaints – if a learner has made a complaint about a particular assessment method or the way you have treated them, you must remain objective and not take anything personally. You should not let this influence any future decisions, however, you could ask if another assessor could take on this learner if you feel uncomfortable with the situation.

- Consistency – are you being fair to all your learners or are you biased towards some learners more than others?

- Methods of assessment – have you used appropriate or alternative methods, for example, asking oral questions rather than issuing written questions for a learner with dyslexia?

- Plagiarism – have any learners copied work from others or the internet, or not referenced their research adequately? You could type a sentence of their work into a search engine to see if it already exists elsewhere.

- Pressure – do you feel under pressure to pass learners who are border-line, perhaps due to funding measures, targets, inspectors or employer expectations?

- Risk assessments – are any of your learners likely to leave, or do they need extra support for any reason? Don't feel obliged to give too much support, to the extent that your learner's work becomes your own.

- The assessment requirements – have both you and your learner inter-preted these in the same way – was the activity too easy or too hard?

- Trends – is there a pattern, i.e. are most learners making the same mis-takes? If so, it could be that they have misinterpreted something or you have misinformed them or been vague or ambiguous. If this is the case, you could summarise the trends and discuss them with your learners. You could also discuss aspects of good practice to further their development.

- Type of assessment – i.e. formal or informal assessments – you might be more lenient with informal assessments to encourage them. However, you do need to be fair and ethical with all your methods and decisions, for example, regarding safety and confidentiality.

- VACSR – is your learner's evidence valid, authentic, current, sufficient and reliable? How can you ensure their work meets all these points? If you are assessing group work, how do you know what each individual has contributed? If you don't know, you might be attributing achieve-ment to those who haven't contributed.

If you are in any doubt, you must talk to someone else who is a specialist in your subject area such as another assessor. Samples of your decisions should be checked by your internal quality assurer to ensure you are assessing correctly and are consistent and fair. However, this usually takes place after you have made a decision and it might be too late if you have made a positive judgement. You will then need to explain to your learner that they have not passed and that they need to do further work. If you are assessing an accredited qualification, an external quality assurer from the awarding organisation for your subject may also sample your decisions and the learner's work. If your learners are working towards an accred-ited qualification, you will need to ensure they have been registered with the appropriate awarding organisation. It might not be your responsibil-ity to carry out this task, but you should communicate the details of your learners to the relevant staff. You should then receive a list of registration numbers which can be added to your assessment documentation.

Ensuring you choose the right method of assessment to carry out with your learners, and making a decision which is fair and ethical will help your learners successfully achieve.

Extension Activity

Consider what could influence you when making an assessment decision. Are the assessment requirements explicit, enabling you to be totally objective, or could they be misinterpreted, making it difficult for you to make a judgement? What would you do if you felt under pressure to pass a learner who had not met the assessment criteria?

Agree an assessment plan with a learner, assess them and make a decision. Then consider if you would do anything differently and why.

Providing feedback to learners and others

All learners need to know how they are progressing and what they have achieved at regular points. Feedback will help encourage, motivate and develop them further. This can be given after an assessment activity, perhaps verbally to your learner; however, it should always be formally documented. When giving feedback in writing, it should be written on the correct document, not just written on your learner's work in case they lose it. You can, of course, make developmental notes on your learner's work, for example, to correct spelling errors, or to make annotations to show you have read it. You must keep records of feedback to show who has achieved what, as well as to satisfy internal and external organisation requirements.

Feedback should be based on facts which relate to what has been assessed and should not be based purely on your personal opinions. The former is known as *objective*, the latter *subjective*. However, you can mix the two. For example, *Well done Tricia, you have met the criteria and I felt the way you handled the situation was really professional.*

The advantages of giving feedback are:

- it creates opportunities for clarification, discussion and progression

- it emphasises progress rather than failure

- it can boost your learner's confidence and motivation

- it identifies further learning opportunities or actions required

- your learner knows what they have achieved

- your learner knows what they need to do to improve or change.

If you are writing feedback to be read by learners at a later date, you need to appreciate that how you write it may not be how they read it. It is easy to interpret words or phrases differently to what is intended; therefore, if you can, read the feedback to them at the time of returning their work to allow a two-way discussion to take place. If you don't see your learners regularly, you could e-mail feedback to them. If so, don't get too personal with this, keep to the facts but be as positive as possible to retain their motivation. If you are giving individual verbal feedback, consider when and where you will do this, so as not to embarrass your learner in any way, and to allow enough time for any questions they may have.

Verbal feedback should be a two-way process, allowing a discussion to take place to clarify any points and plan further actions if necessary. Consider your tone of voice and take into account your learner's non-verbal signals and your own body language. You might give feedback to a group regarding an activity; if so, make sure your feedback is specific to the group, and/or each individual's contributions. Your learners will like to know how they are progressing, and what they need to do to improve or develop further. Simple statements such as 'well done' or 'good' don't tell your learner what was well done or good about their work or how they can improve it. Using your learner's name makes the feedback more personal, being specific enables your learner to see what they need to do to improve, and smiling while giving feedback can be encouraging.

Example

Rashid sees his learners once a month in their work environment to assess their performance. He also sees them once a fortnight in college to support them with their knowledge. Between these times, he marks their assignments and e-mails informal feedback to them. A typical e-mail reads: Paula, you have passed your assignment. I particularly liked the way you compared and contrasted the two theories. Do be careful when proofreading, you tend to use 'were' instead of 'where'. I will return your assignment when I next see you, along with more detailed written feedback.

This feedback is specific and developmental and will help Rashid's learners to stay motivated until he next sees them. Giving feedback this way is also a good method of keeping in touch if you don't see your learners frequently, and gives your learners the opportunity to communicate with you if necessary. E-mails and written feedback enable you to maintain records, if required, for audit purposes. Feedback can lose its impact if you leave it too long, and learners may think you are not interested in their progress if they don't hear from you.

Feedback should always be:

- based on facts and not opinions

- clear, genuine and unambiguous

- constructive and developmental – giving examples for improvement or further development

- documented – records must be maintained

- focused on the activity not the person

- helpful and supportive

- honest, specific and detailed regarding what was or wasn't achieved.

Activity

Think of an instance where you have given feedback recently. How did you do this and could you have improved it in any way? What did you find difficult about giving feedback and why? What records did you maintain and why?

There could be issues such as not having enough time to write detailed feedback, not being very good with eye contact when giving verbal feedback, or not being able to turn negative points into constructive points. Giving feedback which is constructive and helpful to your learners will come with practice. Coffield states:

> If rich feedback is to be given to all learners, then tutors need the time to read and reflect on their assignments, time to write encouraging and stretching comments, and time to discuss these face to face.   (2008, page 36)

If you don't take the time to support your learners with encouraging feedback, you will not be helping them to improve in the long term.

The role of questioning in feedback allows your learner to consider their achievements before you tell them. A good way to do this is to ask your learner how they feel they have done straight after you have assessed them. This gives them the opportunity to recognise their own mistakes, or reflect on what they could have done differently. You could then build on this through feedback, and discuss what needs to be improved and achieved next.

Having good listening skills will help you engage your learners in a conversation by hearing what they are saying, and responding to any questions or concerns. Giving your learners time to talk will encourage them to inform you of things they might not otherwise have said, for example, if something has had an effect upon their progress. Listening for key words will help you focus upon what is being said, for example, *I struggled with the last part of the assignment.* The key word is *struggled* and you could therefore ask a question such as, *What was it that made you struggle?* This would allow a conversation to then take place, giving you the opportunity to help and motivate your learner.

When questioning:

- allow enough time for your questions and your learner's responses
- ask open questions, e.g. beginning with *who, what, when, where, why* and *how*
- avoid trick or complex questions
- be aware of your posture, gestures and body language
- be conscious of your dialect, accent, pitch and tone
- don't ask more than one question in the same sentence
- involve everyone if you are talking to a group
- make sure you don't use closed questions to illicit a *yes* response; learners may feel that is what you want to hear but it doesn't confirm knowledge
- use active listening skills
- try not to say *erm, yeah, okay, you know,* or *does that make sense?*
- use eye contact and smile
- use learners' names
- watch your learners' reactions.

Questioning and feedback should always be adapted to the level of your learners. You won't help your learners if you are using higher level words or jargon when their level of understanding is lower. You should also be aware of where you give the feedback, in case you are interrupted or are in a noisy environment. You should always give feedback in a way which will make it clear how your learner has met the requirements, and what they need to do next.

Example

Hannah is working towards the Certificate in Customer Service. She has just been observed by her assessor Geoff, who has also marked her responses to the written questions. Geoff gave her verbal feedback stating: Hannah, you've done really well and passed all the criteria for the observation and written questions. You dealt with the irate customer in a pleasant and calm way. However, I would recommend you use the customer's name a bit more when speaking with them to appear friendly. You've met all the requirements; we can now sign that unit off and plan for the next one.

In this example, the assessor was constructive, specific and developmental with his feedback; Hannah knew that she had achieved the unit, and what she could do to improve for the future. The use of the word *however* is much better than the word *but*, which can sound negative. The feedback was also worded at the right level for the learner.

Often, the focus of feedback is likely to be on mistakes rather than strengths. If something positive is stated first, any negative comments are more likely to be listened to and acted upon. Starting with a negative point may discourage your learner from listening to anything else that is said. If possible, start with something positive, then state what could be improved, and finish on a developmental note. This sandwiches the negative aspect between two positive or helpful aspects. You will need to find out if your organisation has any specific feedback methods they wish you to use, which will ensure a standardised approach across all assessors to all learners. Whatever method you use to give feedback, it should always be backed up by a written record.

The example in Table 2.3 overleaf is of a *feedback and action* record. It clearly shows what was carried out, what action needs to be taken and what has been achieved. A copy should be given to the learner.

Example

Feedback and action record			
Learner: Irene Jones		Assessor: Jenny Smith	
Qualification: Certificate in Hospitality & Catering		Level: 1	
Aspects assessed	Feedback	Action required (assessment plan to be updated)	Target date
Unit 101 Maintenance of a safe, hygienic and secure working environment	I observed Irene on 6 February at the County Leisure Centre to assess her competence in the workplace. I used the awarding organisation's checklists to ensure all the requirements were met and made additional comments regarding what was seen. Irene successfully performed all the requirements of unit 101 and I am pleased to say she has passed. I also asked some oral questions to check her knowledge and have digitally recorded these as evidence of achievement. I held a discussion with Irene based on the knowledge requirements, which was also digitally recorded. Irene obtained a witness testimony from her supervisor, which confirmed she had successfully covered the criteria over a period of time.	Irene and I will meet on 6 April to complete an assessment plan for unit 102 and review her progress to date. In the meantime, Irene will read the supporting handouts for unit 102 and put theory into practice at the Leisure Centre.	06 April
Achievements: Unit 101	Learning outcomes: 1. Be able to maintain personal health and hygiene. 2. Know how to maintain personal health and hygiene. 3. Be able to help maintain a hygienic, safe and secure workplace. 4. Know how to maintain a hygienic, safe and secure workplace.	Assessment criteria: 1.1 – 1.5 2.1 – 2.5 3.1 – 3.5 4.1 – 4.19	
Signed assessor: J Smith Date: 06 February 12			
Signed learner: I Jones Date: 06 February 2012			
Countersignature and date (if required):			

Table 2.3: Feedback and action record

Different feedback methods include the following:

- Descriptive – describes examples of what could be improved and why, and is usually formal. Using this method lets you describe what your learner has done, how they have achieved the required assessment requirements and what they can do to progress further.

- Evaluative – usually just a statement such as *well done* or *good*. This method does not offer helpful or constructive advice and is usually informal. It does not give learners the opportunity to know what was done well or how they could improve.

- Constructive – is specific and focused to confirm your learner's achievement or to give developmental points in a positive and helpful way.

- Destructive – relates to improvements which are needed and is often given in a negative way which could demoralise your learner.

- Objective – clearly relates to specific assessment requirements and is factual regarding what has and has not been met.

- Subjective – is often just a personal opinion and can be biased, for example, if the assessor is friendly with the learner. Feedback might be vague and not based on the assessment requirements.

When giving feedback to learners you need to be aware that it could affect their self-esteem and whether they continue or not. The quality of feedback received can be a key factor in their progress and the ability to learn new skills and knowledge. Ongoing constructive feedback which has been carefully thought through is an indication of your interest in your learner, and of your intention to help them develop and do well in the future.

When giving feedback:

- own your statements by beginning with the word *I* rather than *you* (however written feedback could be given in the third person if your organisation prefers)

- start with something positive, for example, *I really liked the confident manner in which you delivered your presentation*

- be specific about what you have seen, for example, *I felt the way you explained the law of gravity was really interesting due to your knowledge and humour* or *I found the way you explained the law of gravity was rather confusing to me*

- offer constructive and specific follow-on points, for example, *I feel I would have understood it better if you had broken the subject down into smaller stages*

- end with something positive or developmental, for example, *I enjoyed your presentation – you had prepared well and came across as very organised and professional.* Or *I enjoyed your session, however, a handout summarising the key points would be really helpful to refer to in future.*

Being constructive, specific and developmental with what you say, and owning your statements by beginning with the word *I* should help your learner focus upon what you are saying, and listen to how they can improve. If you don't have any follow-on points then don't create them just for the sake of it. Conversely, if you do have any negative points or criticisms, don't say *My only negative point is ...* or *My only criticisms are ...* It's much better to replace these words and say *Some areas for development could be ...* instead.

If assessment decisions count towards the achievement of a qualification, it is crucial to keep your feedback records, along with any action identified for each learner. Records must always be kept safe and secure; your car boot is not a good idea, nor is a corner of the staffroom or an open-plan office. Awarding organisations expect records to be securely managed, whether they are manual or electronic.

You might need to give feedback to other people, for example, your learner's supervisor in their work environment. You need to be careful of what you say and how you say it. Your feedback could be used as part of the staff appraisal process to monitor your learner's performance and job prospects.

Extension Activity

Compare and contrast different feedback methods such as descriptive and evaluative, constructive and destructive, objective and subjective. Which do you feel you will use when giving feedback in different situations and why?

Standardising practice

Standardisation ensures consistency and fairness of all assessment decisions. It should also give a consistent experience to all learners from the time they commence to the time they leave. You may have to standardise your decisions with other assessors, particularly where more than one assessor is involved with the same subject. It is also an opportunity to ensure all assessors are interpreting the qualification and assessment requirements accurately, and completing records appropriately. Attending a standardisation event will give you the opportunity to share good practice and compare your assessment decisions with your colleagues', by looking at their assessed work and vice versa. You can then discuss your findings as a team. This will ensure you have interpreted the requirements accurately, that the learner evidence is appropriate and that the assessment records are correctly completed. Even if you don't learn anything new, it will confirm you are doing things right.

The example in Table 2.4 below is a standardisation record for reviewing assessed work.

Example

Standardisation record for assessed work			
Learner:	Registration no.:		
Qualification:	Level:		
Standardising assessor:	Original assessor:		
Aspect/s standardised, e.g. unit number:			
Checklist	Yes	No	Action required
Is there an agreed assessment plan with SMART targets?			
Are the assessment methods appropriate and sufficient? Which methods were used?			
Does the evidence meet ALL the required criteria?			
Does the evidence meet VACSR?			
Is there a feedback record clearly showing what has been achieved? (Is it adequate and developmental?)			
Has subsequent action been identified? (if applicable)			
Do you agree with the assessment decision?			
Are all relevant documents signed and dated? (including countersignatures if applicable?)			
Are original assessment records stored separately from the learner's work?			
Comments from original assessor in response to the above:			
Signed (standardising assessor):		Date:	
Signed (original assessor):		Date:	
Key: SMART: specific, measurable, achievable, realistic, time bound VACSR: valid, authentic, current, sufficient, reliable			

Table 2.4: Standardisation record for assessed work

Standardisation events are not team meetings; the latter are to discuss issues relating to the management of the programme, for example, awarding organisation updates, targets, success rates and learner issues. You could also standardise your practice virtually or electronically by reviewing qualification requirements or documents online.

The benefits of standardisation are:

- a consistent experience for all learners
- a contribution to CPD
- accountability to awarding organisations and regulatory authorities
- all assessment decisions are fair for all learners
- an opportunity to discuss changes and developments
- clearly defined roles and responsibilities
- compliance with relevant codes of practice
- confirming your own practice
- consistency and fairness of judgements and decisions
- empowerment of assessors
- ensuring the assessment requirements are followed
- sharing good practice
- spotting trends or inconsistencies
- succession planning if assessors are due to leave
- to maintain an audit trail of aspects standardised
- to give assessors time to formally meet
- to meet quality assurance requirements
- to set action plans for the development of systems and staff.

Example

Lukas was a new assessor, and was not very familiar with the standards of the qualification he was due to assess. The full team of assessors met once a fortnight to discuss the content of each unit. This ensured they were all interpreting the requirements in the same way and making correct decisions. Lukas attended the next meeting and was given the opportunity to reassess a unit which had already been assessed by someone else. This activity helped him understand the requirements and see how the documentation should be completed.

If you assess a vocational qualification, you might decide to carry out three observations with each of your learners, and give them a written test, whereas another assessor might only carry out one observation and ask some verbal questions. Standardising this approach between all assessors ensures the process is fair. There are times when an individual learner's needs should be taken into account, which will lead to a difference in assessment activities. However, all learners should be entitled to the same assessment experience, no matter to which assessor they are allocated.

Standardised summative assessments, marked in the same way for every-one, are necessary for any modern society, which aspires to fairness and justice for its citizens. (Wolf, 2008, page 19)

Ways to standardise practice include:

- comparing how documents have been completed

- designing or revising documents

- ensuring the same documents are used by everyone

- judging evidence as a team rather than by one assessor

- looking at the qualification standards and discussing how each assessor interprets them and what they would expect from their learners

- remarking or reassessing work to ensure the same decision is reached

- peer observations/shadowing

- role-playing aspects such as assessment planning, making a decision and giving feedback (these could be recorded to allow playback, pauses and discussions)

- writing assessment materials as a team to ensure all learners are given a fair chance, for example, assignments

- writing questions along with expected responses.

Records should also be maintained of all standardisation activities.

It's important to keep up to date with any changes to what you are assess-ing. If you are assessing an accredited qualification, the standards will change every few years. Awarding organisations issue regular updates, either by hard copy or electronically. Once you receive these, you need to discuss the content with your colleagues to ensure you all interpret them the same way. It would prove useful to maintain minutes of meetings reflecting your responses to changes and updates.

Obtaining feedback

Obtaining the views of your learners and others will greatly assist you when reflecting upon your role as an assessor, and aid the standardisation process. You could ask your learners directly after an assessment activity how they felt the process went. However, while some learners might feel confident enough to tell you, others might not. When evaluating your own practice, you need to consider the views of your learners and others in order to improve. How you do this will depend upon the type of feedback you have obtained and how useful it will be.

A survey might have ascertained that most learners felt the initial assessment could be improved, for example, a computerised learning styles test rather than a paper-based one. You might have obtained feedback from an individual learner that their assessment plan had unrealistic target dates. In this case, you could renegotiate the plan with more suitable dates. Feedback from your learners might impact upon your role by enlightening you to other aspects, for example, the types of questions used in an assignment were too complex, some activities might not have been challenging enough, or a multiple-choice test confused a learner with dyslexia as they mistook a *b* for a *d*.

Feedback will help standardise the practice of assessors by ensuring the activities used are valid and reliable and the assessment types and methods are safe and fair. The views of your learners and others should have an impact upon your own role by helping you improve the assessment experience for your learners.

Extension Activity

Look at the standardisation form in Table 2.4. Does your organisation use something similar? If not, use this form to ensure you are standardising your judgements with other assessors the next time you meet. You would need to take along all your records as well as your learner's evidence. After using it, analyse what changes you would make to the form or the standardisation process.

Record keeping – assessment

It is important to keep records, otherwise how can you prove what your learners have achieved? You also need to satisfy any company, quality assurance, awarding organisation or regulatory authorities' audit requirements. This will usually be for a set period, for example three years, and should be the original records, not photocopies or carbon copies. It is fine to give copies to your learners, as it is harder to forge a copy than an original. Sadly, there are learners who do this; therefore keeping the originals will ensure your records are authentic.

When learners submit work, for example, an assignment, it is good practice to issue a receipt. If not, a learner might say that they have submitted their work when they haven't.

Keeping full and accurate factual records is also necessary in case one of your learners appeals against an assessment decision. If this happens, don't take it personally – they will be appealing against your decision, not you. You will also need to pass records to your internal quality assurer if necessary and any other authorised colleagues who have an interest in your learner's progress and achievement.

The types of assessment records you might maintain include:	You might also use and need to maintain other records such as:
• achievement dates and grades, e.g. pass/refer • assessment plan and review records • assessment tracking sheet showing achievement of all learners • diagnostic test results • discussion records • feedback and action records • initial assessment records • learning styles results • observation checklists and reports • performance and knowledge records • progress reports • records of achievement • records of oral questions and responses • standardisation records.	• action plans • appeals records • application forms • audio/digital/video recordings • authentication statements • CPD records • copies of certificates • enrolment forms • personal details of learners • receipts for assignments • register or record of attendance • retention, success and achievement records • tutorial reviews • unit declarations • witness testimonies.

Table 2.5: Types of assessment records

There may be a standardised approach to completing the records, for example, the amount of detail which must be written, or whether the records should be completed manually or electronically. You will need to find out what your organisation expects you to do. Some organisations now use handheld devices to directly input information and support their learners to produce their work electronically, for example, an e-portfolio of evidence.

All records should be kept secure and should only be accessible by relevant staff. You also need to ensure you comply with organisational and statutory guidelines such as the Data Protection Act (2003) and the Freedom of Information Act (2000).

Some records might be maintained centrally within your organisation using a management information system. These should include:

- appeals and complaints
- assessor details: name, contact information, curriculum vitae, CPD plans and records
- awarding organisation qualification handbook
- enrolment, and/or unique learner number
- equal opportunities data such as an analysis of learners by ethnic origin, disability, gender and age, etc.
- evaluation forms, questionnaire and survey results
- internal and external quality assurance reports
- learner details: name, address, date of birth, contact information, registration
- organisational self-assessment report
- records of actions taken from the above reports
- regulatory and funding guidance
- schemes of work and session plans for taught programmes
- statistics such as retention, success, achievement and destinations.

The Data Protection Act (2003) is mandatory for all organisations that hold or process personal data. The Act contains eight principles, to ensure that data are:

1. processed fairly and lawfully

2. obtained and used only for specified and lawful purposes

3. adequate, relevant and not excessive

4. accurate and, where necessary, kept up to date

5. kept for no longer than necessary

6. processed in accordance with the individual's rights

7. kept secure

8. transferred only to countries that offer adequate protection.

Confidentiality should be maintained regarding all information you keep. The Freedom of Information Act (2000) gives your learners the opportunity to request to see the information public authorities hold about them. All external stakeholders such as awarding organisations and funding bodies should be aware of your systems of record-keeping as they may need to approve certain records or storage methods.

All records should be accurate and legible. If you need to make any amendments, make crossings out rather than use correction fluid. Try to keep on top of your paperwork, even if this is carried out electronically. If you leave it a while, you may forget to note important points. You will need to be organised and have a system; learner records could be stored alphabetically in a filing cabinet, or in separate electronic folders on a computer. If storing electronically, make sure you keep a back-up copy in case anything gets deleted accidentally. Other records could be stored by the programme or qualification title, awarding organisation name, etc.

Example

Andrea has a group of 12 learners working towards a Certificate in Health and Social Care. She maintains an A4 lever arch file, which has a tracking sheet at the front to record the dates of each learner's completed units. She then has plastic wallets for each learner, filed alphabetically, which contain their assessment plans and reviews, skills and knowledge reports, along with feedback and action records. She has a separate folder for the awarding organisation standards and templates. As she manually completes a document, she makes a carbon copy to give to her learners.

When completing any records, if signatures are required, these should be obtained as soon as possible after the event if they cannot be signed on the day. Any signatures added later should have the date they were added, rather than the date the form was originally completed. If you are assessing your learners directly, for example, by an observation, you will know who they are. If you are assessing work that has been handed to you on a different date, or sent electronically, you will need to ensure it is the work of your learner.

If you are assessing a programme which is not accredited by an awarding organisation, you will need to follow the requirements for *recognising and recording progress and achievement in non-accredited learning* (RARPA). There are five processes to RARPA.

1. Aims – these should be appropriate to the individual or group of learners.

2. Initial assessment – this should be used to establish each learner's starting point.

3. Identification of appropriately challenging learning objectives – these should be agreed, renegotiated and revised as necessary after formative assessment, and should be appropriate to each learner.

4. Recognition and recording of progress and achievement during the programme – this should include assessor feedback, learner reflection and reviews of progress.

5. End of programme – this includes summative assessment, learner self-assessment and a review of overall progress and achievement. This should be in relation to the learning objectives and any other outcomes achieved during the programme.

If you use the RARPA system, you will need to check what records must be maintained; there may be a standard system for you to follow or you may need to design your own assessment records.

Record keeping and ensuring the authenticity of your learners' work is of paramount importance. To satisfy everyone involved in the assessment process you must be able to show a valid audit trail for all your decisions.

A useful record to track overall learner progress is known as an assessment tracking sheet. Table 2.6 on page 81 is an example.

Example

Assessment tracking sheet						
Assessor: Jenny Smith			Qualification: Level 1 Certificate in Hospitality & Catering			
Learner and registration number:	Aspects assessed:	101	102	103	104	105
Chang Hanadi 4524UDBQ		11/06/12 Pass		08/03/12 Pass	10/05/12 Refer 15/05/12 Pass	
Hamed Aamir 1674UEME			07/05/12 Pass			
Jones Irene 1234ABCD		06/02/12 Pass				
Wilson Peter 7985IENF		15/01/12 Pass	04/02/12 Pass			
Young Lou 7496UWME		10/01/12 Pass				

Table 2.6: Assessment tracking sheet

Portfolios of evidence

Some qualifications require learners to produce a portfolio of evidence. A portfolio is a record of evidence which proves achievement and can be manual or electronic. It is an ideal opportunity for learners to holistically cross-reference the evidence they provide across several areas. There's no need for them to produce evidence for all the assessment criteria; they can just give the piece of evidence a number and quote this number against the relevant assessment criteria it meets. If this is the case, your learner should have a copy of the qualification's requirements to help them see what is involved. You can both refer to these when planning the types of evidence which will be provided, and how and when you will assess the evidence.

With any portfolio, the quality of the evidence is important, not the quantity. When you are assessing evidence, you don't want to be spending a lot of time searching for something and your internal quality assurer won't want to either. Some qualifications might require you, as the assessor, to cross-reference the evidence rather than the learner. If this is the case, you will need to plan what is required and by when, encouraging your learner to self-assess their evidence towards the relevant assessment criteria before giving it to you. Your assessment records should be kept independently from your learners' portfolios. However, you should give copies to your learners as evidence of the assessment process taking place.

Electronic portfolios, known as e-portfolios, are becoming more popular as learners can generate and upload their evidence at a time to suit. Often the qualification standards are already within the online system and will automatically cross-reference the evidence to the criteria. Some systems also allow communication to take place between assessors and learners and track all contact. Evidence can be in the form of data files, scanned documents, video and audio files, etc. Assessment of evidence can therefore take place remotely. Assessment in the form of an observation might still be necessary; although this could be digitally recorded and/or observed via a web camera. When assessing electronic evidence, you must make sure that it has been produced solely by your learner. Your assessment records and feedback can also be uploaded to the system.

Extension Activity

Locate your organisation's documentation which you will be required to use during the assessment process. How does it differ to the examples in this chapter? What changes would you recommend to it and why?

Summary

In this chapter you have learnt about:

- assessment planning in the work environment
- making assessment decisions
- providing feedback to learners and others
- standardising practice
- record keeping – assessment.

Evidence from the completed activities, plus the following, could be used towards the *Assessing occupational competence in the work environment* unit, for example:

- four completed assessment plans for at least two learners (methods must include observation of performance, examining work products and questions – to be assessed in the work environment)

- four assessment activities you would use with your learners (e.g. observation checklists, assignments, written questions, oral questions)

- four completed feedback records for the two learners

- minutes of assessor team meetings

- records of standardisation

- written statements cross-referenced to the TAQA unit's assessment criteria

- answers to questions issued by the awarding organisation

- records of discussions with your assessor.

Cross-referencing grid

This chapter contributes towards the following three TAQA units' assessment criteria. Full details of the learning outcomes and assessment criteria for each TAQA unit can be found in the Appendices.

TAQA unit	Assessment criteria
Understanding the principles and practices of assessment	3.1, 3.2 4.2 5.1, 5.2 6.2 7.2 8.2
Assess occupational competence in the work environment	1.1, 1.2, 1.3, 1.4 2.1, 2.2, 2.3, 2.4 3.1, 3.2, 3.3
Assess vocational skills, knowledge and understanding	1.1, 1.3 2.4, 2.5, 2.6 3.1, 3.2, 3.3

Theory focus

References and further information

Coffield, F (2008) *Just Suppose Teaching and Learning Became the First Priority*. London: LSN.

LLUK (2007) *Addressing Literacy, Language, Numeracy and ICT Needs in Education and Training: Defining the Minimum Core of Teachers' Knowledge, Understanding and Personal Skills*. London: Lifelong Learning UK.

Ofqual (2009) *Authenticity – A Guide for Teachers*. Coventry: Ofqual.

Pachler, N et al. (2009) *Scoping a vision for formative e-assessment* (FEASST) JISC.

Race, P, Brown, S and Smith, B (2004) 500 *Tips on Assessment*. Abingdon: Routledge.

Tummons, J (2011) *Assessing Learning in the Lifelong Learning Sector* (3rd edition). Exeter: Learning Matters.

Wolf, A (2008) Looking for the best result. *Make the Grade*, Summer 2008. Institute of Educational Assessors.

Websites

Assessment methods: www.brookes.ac.uk/services/ocsid/resources/methods.html

Assessment resources: www.excellencegateway.org.uk and www.questionmark.co.uk

Data Protection Act (2003): http://regulatorylaw.co.uk/Data_Protection_Act_2003.html

Efutures (e-assessment regulators): www.ofqual.gov.uk/how-we-regulate/90-articles/7-e-assessment

Freedom of Information Act (2000): www.legislation.gov.uk/ukpga/2000/36/contents

Health and Safety Executive: www.hse.gov.uk

Learning Records Service: www.learningrecordsservice.org.uk

Learning Styles: www.vark-learn.com

Oxford Learning Institute: Giving and receiving feedback – www.learning.ox.ac.uk/supervision/stages/feedback/

Plagiarism: www.plagiarism.org and www.plagiarismadvice.org

QCF shortcut: http://tinyurl.com/2944r8h

RARPA: www.learningcurve.org.uk/resources/learning/rarpa

Introduction

In this chapter you will learn about:

- assessment planning in other contexts

- managing and reviewing the assessment process

- a range of questioning techniques

- the role of ICT in assessment

- continuing professional development (CPD)

There are activities and examples which will help you reflect on the above and will assist your knowledge of how to assess vocational skills, knowledge and understanding. Completing the activities will help you to gather evidence towards the TAQA *Assessing vocational skills, knowledge and understanding* unit. At the end of each section is an extension activity to stretch and challenge your learning further.

At the end of the chapter is a list of possible evidence which could be used towards the TAQA *Assessing vocational skills, knowledge and understanding* unit.

A cross-referencing grid shows how the content of this chapter contributes towards the three TAQA units' assessment criteria. There is also a theory focus with relevant references, further information and websites to which you might like to refer.

Assessment planning in other contexts

If you are assessing an academic or vocational programme, you might also be teaching it, for example in a classroom or training organisation. This would enable you to get to know your learners before you assess them. Conversely, someone else might teach the learners and you might just be responsible for assessing their learning. Teaching and assessment can take place in many contexts, for example, a college, training organisation, prison, community hall or other appropriate location.

When planning assessment activities, you need to know when your learners are ready. There's no point assessing them if they haven't learnt everything they need to know, as you will be setting them up to fail. If you don't teach the learners that you will assess, you will need to communicate with the person who has taught them to ensure the required learning has taken place.

If a learner has been absent for any reason, make sure they are up to date regarding what they have missed. Carrying out a formative assessment well before a summative assessment can help both you and your learner see how ready they are.

The timing of your assessments can also make a difference: if you plan to assess on a Friday before a holiday period, your learners might not be as attentive; equally so first thing on a Monday morning. This is difficult, of course, if you only see your learners on these particular days. If you are planning a schedule of assessments throughout the year, you will need to consider any public or cultural holidays. There is no point planning to assess on Mondays if the majority of these fall on public holidays.

You will need to carry out some form of assessment planning with your learners, even if it's just agreeing target dates for the submission of assignments or planning the dates of tests. Your learners need to know what they are working towards, i.e. the programme or qualification content, and when and how they will be assessed, for example, by assignments. This could be in the form of an action plan rather than an assessment plan. The action plan would contain the titles of the assignments; however, further guidance should be given as to the expected content and word counts, etc. The action plan can be updated with achievement dates, and added to or amended as necessary. See Chapter 2 for further details regarding assessment planning. An example action plan is shown in Table 3.1 opposite.

If you are teaching as well as assessing, you will need to prepare a scheme of work to show what you will teach and when, and how you will assess skills, knowledge and understanding. For example, formative assessments could be quizzes, multiple choice tests, role plays, etc. Summative assessments could be assignments, exams or tests. When planning your programme delivery, make sure you have taught all the required material before carrying out summative assessments. Ongoing formative assessments will help you gauge that learning has taken place. You will need to ensure appropriate time is planned for assessment activities during your sessions, or in between (i.e. as homework), along with time for you to give feedback.

Example

Action plan			
Learner:	Marcia Indira	Assessor: Abbi Cross	
Qualification and level:	Level 2 Business, Administration and Finance	Registration number: 7913PIRW	
Date commenced:	5 September 2011	Expected completion date: 28 July 2012	
Assignment	Assignment questions	Target date	Achievement date
Unit 1: Business Enterprise Learning outcome 2: Be able to develop a business enterprise idea	Q1 – Generate a range of ideas for a business enterprise	7 October 2011	
	Q2 – Compare the viability of the business enterprise ideas	14 October 2011	
	Q3 – Select and develop a business idea	21 October 2011	

Table 3.1: Example action plan

If you are teaching as well as assessing, you may need to take an appropriate teaching qualification – see the Introduction for further details. Taking a qualification will help you learn more about schemes of work and session planning.

It could be that your learners will be taking an exam and this will need to be planned and invigilated according to the awarding organisation's requirements on a set date. Some assignments might also need to be completed under supervised conditions. You would therefore need to ensure you have taught everything in good time. You could use past exam papers as a formative assessment activity with your learners beforehand.

If your learners are working towards an accredited qualification, you will need to ensure they have been registered with the appropriate awarding organisation. It might not be your responsibility to carry out this task, but you should communicate the details of your learners to the relevant staff. You should then receive a list of registration numbers which can be added to your assessment documentation.

If a record of attendance or an in-house certificate will be issued to your learners, this information should be communicated to the person who will create them. You should inform your learners when they can expect to receive any feedback or formal recognition of their achievements, and what they can do if they disagree with a decision you have made.

The subject you assess will determine the assessment type and method to be used. For example, an academic programme could be assessed by an exam whereas a vocational programme could be assessed by an observation. You will need to check the syllabus to see what activities are provided for you or what you will have to devise.

Activities can be initial (at the beginning), formative (part way through a programme), and/or summative (at the end of a unit, qualification or programme). Formative assessments will check ongoing progress and usually consist of informal activities. Summative assessments will confirm achievement and usually consist of formal activities. See Chapter 1 for other types of assessment you might wish to use. Assessment activities can be assessor led, e.g. observations, learner led, e.g. assignments, or a mixture of both. The methods will vary depending upon whether you are assessing skills, knowledge or understanding; some methods can cover both. See Chapter 1 Table 1.4 for a more comprehensive list of assessment methods and activities.

Skills	Knowledge and understanding
• assignments • case studies • creating products • discussions • observation in a workshop or a realistic working environment (RWE) • peer assessments • projects (individual or team based) • recognition of prior learning (RPL) • role plays • self-assessments • simulations • skills tests	• assignments • case studies • discussions • exams • oral and written questions • presentations • projects (individual or team based) • puzzles • quizzes • recognition of prior learning (RPL) • reflective learning journals • tests and multiple choice questions • written statements

Table 3.2: Skills, knowledge and understanding

If you are responsible for devising your own assessment methods and activities, you might decide to choose ones which are easy to mark for example multiple choice. You might not have a lot of time for preparation and marking, therefore the more time you spend preparing something suitable and relevant, the easier the marking will be. There's no point making assessment activities complex unless it's a requirement of the qualification or you need to challenge higher level learners. Lower level learners can easily become demoralised if the activities are unattainable.

If you assess group work, such as role play or discussions in a classroom, you need to assess each individual's contribution towards the assessment requirements. Otherwise you could be passing the whole group when some learners may not have contributed much at all. You could design a checklist to help you document who did what to ensure the contribution of everyone is assessed fairly. If you are related to, or know personally, the learners you will assess, you should notify your organisation of any conflict of interest. They may also need to notify the relevant awarding organisation in case you are not allowed to assess a learner if they are a partner, a direct member of your family or your spouse's family.

Whatever subject you are going to assess, you need to ensure your learners have acquired and mastered the knowledge, attitudes and/or skills required at the right level for achievement. There's no point teaching your learners to repeat expected answers or to demonstrate a task if they don't really understand what they are doing and why. When you are devising assessment materials, for example, questions, essays or assignments, you need to pitch these at the correct level for your learners to be able to demonstrate their understanding. If you are assessing an accredited qualification, it will already be assigned a level, for example, *Level 3 Certificate in Hospitality and Catering*. If it's not accredited, you will need to pitch your assessment materials at the level which is suitable for your learners, for example, beginners, intermediate or advanced. Knowing which level you are assessing will help you use the correct level of objectives when writing assessment materials.

Bloom (1956) believed that education should focus on the mastery of subjects and the promotion of higher forms of thinking, rather than an approach which simply transfers facts. His taxonomy model of classification places learning into three overlapping domains. These are:

1. the cognitive domain (intellectual capability, i.e. knowledge or thinking)

2. the affective domain (feelings, emotions and behaviour, i.e. attitudes or beliefs)

3. the psychomotor domain (manual and physical skills, i.e. skills or actions).

The three domains are summarised as *knowledge, attitudes* and *skills*, or *think, feel, do*. Your learners should benefit from the development of knowledge and intellect (cognitive domain); attitudes and beliefs (affective domain); and the ability to put physical skills into practice (psychomotor domain). You would therefore assess your learners at the right level for their learning, at the appropriate time. Each domain contains objectives at different levels, such as *list, describe, explain,* and *analyse.* You will see these objectives in the qualification handbook for your subject, often referred to as *assessment criteria.* If the qualification you are assessing is on the Qualifications and Credit Framework (QCF), it will be at a particular level (from foundation level to level 8) depending upon the subject and your learners.

Example

Pierre has a group of level 1 learners working towards a Certificate in Engineering. He carries out formative assessment of his learners using objectives such as state (to test knowledge), familiarise (to test attitudes), and use (to test skills). When he is sure his learners have mastered the topics, he will give them a summative test which will assess the required knowledge, attitudes and skills needed to achieve the Certificate.

If Pierre used objectives such as *justify* and *facilitate*, these would be too high a level for his learners to achieve. If his learners progress to level 2, Pierre could then use objectives relevant to that level such as *describe* and *demonstrate.*

If you are assessing a qualification which is on the QCF, there will be specific learning outcomes to help you plan what you will teach, and assessment criteria for your learners to achieve. If a qualification is offered at different levels, often the learning outcomes are the same, but the assessment criteria are different. The latter might use objectives such as *describe* for a lower level, *explain* for an intermediate level and *analyse* for a higher level. The content of the qualification remains the same; the difference is in the amount of work the learners will do to achieve a higher level. However, learners will often feel they are capable of achieving a higher level, even though that might not be the case.

Example

Elaine is assessing the Award in Preparing to Teach in the Lifelong Learning Sector. She has a mixed group of level 3 and level 4 learners. All of the learners opt to take the level 4 assessments. However, once Elaine assesses their responses, she realises most of them only meet the criteria for level 3. When she informs them of this, they do not take the feedback well.

In this example, all the learners felt they were capable of a higher level of achievement, and were therefore demoralised when told they were not up to the required standard. If an initial assessment had been carried out, the learners would have been aware of their abilities and which level to work towards.

If you have a mixed group of learners you could adapt your formative assessment activities to reflect what *everyone* should achieve, what *most* will achieve and what *some* will achieve. For example, everyone will *describe*, most will *explain* and some will *analyse*. This is a useful way of challenging more able learners while those less able can still achieve something.

Table 3.3 gives examples of objectives you could use when devising assessment materials at different levels. If you are assessing an accredited qualification, you will need to follow the objectives stated in the assessment criteria.

Level	Skills	Knowledge	Attitudes
Foundation	attempt	list	adopt
I	use	state	familiarise
2	demonstrate	describe	identify
3	assemble	explain	review
4	complete	analyse	discuss
5	establish	evaluate	define
6	utilise	justify	conclude
7	modify	criticise	differentiate
8	operate	redefine	discriminate

Table 3.3: Examples of objectives

Activity

Design four different assessment activities which you could use with your learners. They should be based around the criteria you are going to assess and be at the correct level for your learners. You should create example responses for any questions that you are asking to ensure consistent assessment decisions. If possible, carry out the activities with learners and evaluate their strengths and limitations.

Peer and self-assessment

Peer assessment involves a learner assessing another learner's progress. Self-assessment involves a learner assessing their own progress. Both methods encourage learners to make decisions about what has been learnt so far, and to reflect on aspects for further development. Your learners will need to fully understand the assessment criteria, and how to be analytical and objective with their judgements. Throughout the process of peer and self-assessment, learners can develop skills such as listening, observing and questioning.

Peer assessment can also be useful to develop and motivate learners. However, this should be managed carefully, as you may have some learners who do not get along and might use the opportunity to demoralise one another. You would need to give advice to your learners as to how to give feedback effectively. If learner feedback is given skilfully, other learners may consider more what their peers have said than what you have said. If you consider peer assessment to have a valuable contribution to make to the assessment process, ensure you plan for it to enable your learners to become accustomed and more proficient at giving it. The final decision as to the competence of your learner will lie with you.

Table 3.4 opposite gives the advantages and limitations of each type of assessment.

Boud (1995) suggested that learning and development will not occur without self-assessment and reflection. However, this must be done honestly and realistically if it is going to aid improvement. This process can promote learner involvement and personal responsibility. All learners should be fully aware of the requirements of the qualification and therefore ensure their work is focused towards the assessment criteria.

Peer assessment	
Advantages	**Limitations**
• It can reduce the amount of teacher assessment. • It increases attention for activities such as peer presentations if feedback has to be given. • Learners are more focused upon the assessment criteria. • Learners may accept comments from peers better than those from the assessor. • It promotes learner and peer interaction and involvement.	• All peers should be involved therefore planning needs to take place as to who will give feedback and to whom. • Appropriate conditions are needed. • The assessor needs to confirm each learner's progress and achievements as it might be different from their peers' judgement. • Everyone needs to understand the assessment criteria. • Learners might be subjective and friendly rather than objective with their decisions. • It needs to be carefully managed to ensure there are no personality conflicts or unjustified comments. • It should be supported with other assessment methods. • Some peers may be anxious, nervous or lack confidence to give feedback.
Self-assessment	
Advantages	**Limitations**
• It encourages learners to check their own progress and achievement. • It encourages reflection. • Mistakes can be seen as opportunities. • It promotes learner involvement and personal responsibility.	• The assessor needs to discuss and confirm progress and achievement. • It is difficult to be objective when making a decision. • Learners may feel they have achieved more than they actually have. • Learners must fully understand the assessment criteria. • Learners need to be specific about what they have achieved and what they need to do to complete any gaps. • Some learners may lack confidence in their ability to make decisions about their own progress.

Table 3.4: Peer assessment advantages and limitations

Peer feedback could be written rather than given verbally and therefore be anonymous. This would encourage objective opinions as learners will not feel they are betraying their peers. Ground rules should be established to ensure the process is valid and fair.

Examples of peer and self-assessment activities include learners:

- assessing each other's work anonymously and giving written or verbal feedback

- completing checklists, templates or pro-formas

- giving grades and/or written or verbal feedback regarding own or peer presentations

- holding group discussions before collectively agreeing a grade and giving feedback, perhaps for a presentation

- producing a written statement of how they could improve their own or peers' work

- suggesting improvements to their own or peers' work.

Communicating with others

You will need to communicate with other people who are involved in the assessment process of your learners. You should remain professional at all times as you are representing your organisation. People might not always remember your name, however, you will be known as 'that person from XYZ organisation'. You therefore need to create a good and lasting impression of yourself and your organisation. In some organisations, you may be required to wear a name badge, have identification and sign in and out for security reasons.

You will not have a second chance to make a first impression, therefore it is important to portray yourself in a professional way. That is not only with what you say, but in the way you say it, your attitude, body language and dress. A warm and confident smile, positive attitude, self-assurance and the use of eye contact will all help when communicating, particularly if you are meeting someone for the first time.

You may act differently depending upon the circumstances and who you are with, for example, informally with colleagues or formally with external quality assurers. Communication can be verbal, non-verbal or written. Whichever method you use, communication is a means of passing on information from one person to another.

Skills of communicating effectively include the way you speak, listen and express yourself, for example, with body language and written information. You need to be confident and organised with what you wish to convey; the way you do this will give an impression of yourself for better or worse. You may have to attend meetings or video conferences, and wherever you are with other people, they will make assumptions about you based on what they see and hear. You may have to write reports, memos or e-mails and the way you express yourself when writing is as important as when speaking.

You might need to liaise with support staff within your organisation, perhaps to arrange help with preparing and copying assessment materials and resources, or by making modifications or adaptations to equipment and materials. You might also need to get in touch with others who have an involvement with your learners, for example, parents, probation officers or social workers. If this is the case, remember aspects of confidentiality and data protection, and keep notes of all discussions in case you need to refer to them again.

People you may need to communicate with, besides your learners, are those who are internal and external to your organisation, examples of which are given in Table 3.5 below.

Internal	External
• administrators • assessors • colleagues • exam officers • internal quality assurers • invigilators • managers • mentors • teachers • trainers • support staff	• careers advisers • employers • external quality assurers • inspectors and regulators • parents, guardians or carers • probation officers • social workers • staff from other organisations and agencies • witnesses and others involved in the assessment of your learners

Table 3.5: Internal and external support staff

You might teach a particular subject, but not assess it; for example, your learners may take an exam which is marked by the awarding organisation, or a test which is marked by a colleague. You might have to plan for examinations to take place, in which case you will need to ensure the administration staff are aware of what will take place and when, as invigilators may be needed, and specific rooms timetabled accordingly.

If you are not the only assessor for your subject, you will need to standardise your practice with others. If you are assessing an academic qualification, you might use the term *double marking* rather than standardisation. This enables different assessors to mark one another's assessed work, to ensure the correct grade has been given. This could take place blindly, i.e. you don't get to see the original grade. Having a marking scheme or expected answers will help you reach a fair decision. If standardisation is not carried out, assessment activities will not be fair to all learners.

If you feel it is difficult to make an objective decision with existing assessment activities, you will need to discuss your concerns with other staff, or with a contact from the awarding organisation. You may need to redesign some activities to make them more specific and/or unambiguous. If all your learners are achieving everything with ease, perhaps you need to be more challenging with the tasks you set.

If your subject or qualification is quality assured, your internal and external quality assurers will sample your work to ensure your judgements and decisions are correct and fair. Some learners might have a mentor, someone who is supporting and encouraging them while they go through the learning and assessment process. They may also have other teachers who will assess them. However, do be aware of any sensitive or confidential issues relating to your learners which they may not wish you to pass on. Conversely, you may need to inform others of any particular learner requirements to ensure consistency of support.

If you have learners who are attending a programme in conjunction with a school or other organisation, you may need to liaise with their staff, i.e. to give reports of progress and attendance. You may need to communicate with employers, managers or supervisors whose staff you are assessing in the work environment. If this is the case, make sure you are aware of any protocols involved, and follow your organisation's procedures for dealing with external clients.

Activity

Find out who you need to communicate with, either internally or externally, regarding the subjects you are assessing. How can you contact them and why would you? Make a note of telephone numbers, addresses, websites, e-mail addresses, etc. which could come in useful.

When communicating verbally, your tone, pace and inflections are all important factors in getting your message across. If you speak too quickly or softly, others may not hear everything you say; always try to speak clearly. It is useful to consider what reactions you want to achieve from the information you are communicating, and if others react differently, you will need to amend your methods. You may be communicating via the telephone, therefore unable to see any reactions to your words, which could lead to a misunderstanding. Always ask questions to check that the person you are communicating with has understood what you have said. Non-verbal communication includes your body language and posture, for example, gestures, and the way you stand or sit. Be conscious of your mannerisms, for example, folded arms, hands in pockets, or the gestures you make, etc., and use eye contact with the person you are communicating with. The things you don't say are as important as those you do say.

Written communication, for example, in the form of feedback for assessed work, or an e-mail, is also an expression of you as a person. The way you convey your words and phrases, and your intention, may not be how it is read or understood by the other person. There are always different ways of interpreting the same event. If you are working with learners via an online programme, you may never see them, but will probably build up a visual image; they may therefore be doing the same of you. Information can be easily misinterpreted; therefore the sender has to be sure the receiver will interpret any communication in the way that it was intended. You need to get your message across effectively; otherwise what you are conveying may not necessarily reflect your own thoughts and may cause a breakdown in communication. Any written text cannot be taken back, so there is less room for errors or mistakes and you need to be clear about the exact meaning you wish to convey. Your writing style, words and syntax need checking for spelling, grammar and punctuation. Don't rely on a computer to check these, as it will not always realise the context in which you are writing. This is particularly the case when writing feedback to learners; if you make a spelling mistake, they will think it is correct as you are deemed as the more knowledgeable person.

You might give feedback to your learners via a computer: for example, an e-mail or an e-assessment program. If you use this type of medium for communication and/or assessment purposes, try not to get in the habit of abbreviating words or cutting out vowels. It is important to express yourself in a professional way, otherwise misunderstanding and confusion may arise. Just imagine you are talking to the other person, and type your message appropriately.

Example

Aasif has a good professional working relationship with his group. He needs to e-mail his learners to remind them that the room they will be in next week is to be changed due to examinations taking place in their usual room. He keeps his e-mail brief and to the point by stating: **Hi all, just a quick reminder that we will be in room G3 next week instead of G5, Aasif.** *A poor alternative could have been:* **Hey, I told u last week we wld be in a different room cos of exams, so don't forget where u have to go, and dont get lost, A.**

The latter is unprofessional, is rather negative, contains errors, and doesn't convey where the learners should go. This would not give a good impression, and the learners may lose some respect for their assessor.

If your organisation takes on new assessors, you might be asked to mentor and support them. If they are unqualified and you are already a qualified assessor, you might also be asked to countersign their decisions to ensure they are valid and fair. New staff should be given an induction to the assessment policy and procedures, all relevant paperwork, systems and organisational requirements. If an assessor is leaving, there should be a system of succession planning, to allow time for a successful handover, and any relevant training to take place. Usually, the awarding organisation will need to be informed of any new staff to ensure that they are suitably qualified and experienced.

You could have learners who have excelled in some way, and your organisation or awarding organisation might have an award or medal for which they could be nominated. Your own organisation or department might hold a celebration event to present certificates to successful learners. This is also a way of obtaining positive publicity for your organisation, valuing and celebrating the success of your learners.

Knowing who you need to deal with, how you should proceed, and what is involved in the communication process should make your role as an assessor more rewarding and professional.

Extension Activity

*Research two theories of communication such as Berne's (1973)
Transactional Analysis theory and Belbin's (1993) Team Role Descriptors.
Have a look at their websites and see how the theories have developed
since introduction. Analyse how these theories might impact upon your
role as an assessor as well as the assessment process with your learners.*

Managing and reviewing the assessment process

It is important to review learner progress regularly. This gives you the
opportunity to discuss on a one-to-one basis how your learners are progressing, what they have achieved, and what they may need to do to
improve or work on in the future.

Reviews of progress with learners are part of the assessment process and
provide the opportunity to carry out formative assessments in an informal
way. They also give your learner the opportunity to discuss any concerns or
ask questions they might have been self-conscious about asking in a group
situation. The review should be carried out at a suitable time during the
learning and assessment process and records should be maintained. Informal
reviews and discussions can take place at any opportune time. Reviewing
progress enables you to differentiate effectively, ensuring that the needs of
your learners are met, and that they are being challenged to develop to their
full potential. It also helps ascertain if learners are experiencing any difficulties, enabling you to arrange for any necessary support or further training.

Reviewing learner progress enables you to:

- confirm achievements and plan areas for development
- check skills and knowledge gained from a previous session, before commencing the current session
- discuss any confidential or sensitive issues
- give constructive and developmental feedback
- keep a record of what was discussed
- involve your learners, formally or informally

- motivate your learners

- plan for differentiation

- plan future learning and assessments

- plan more challenging or creative assessment opportunities

- provide opportunities for further learning or support

- review your own contribution to the learning and assessment process

- revise your scheme of work and session plans

- revise your strategies for assessment

- update your learner's assessment or action plan.

If possible, a formal one-to-one review should take place at some point during every programme as it is a key element of the assessment process

Example

Richard has a group of 12 learners who are attending a weekly evening class in pottery from 7 to 9 p.m. for 30 weeks. He has decided to dedicate one session every ten weeks for individual tutorials and reviews. While he is carrying these out, the rest of the group will work on projects or use the organisation's library or computer facilities. This enables Richard to discuss individual progress, concerns and actions with each learner. It also helps him plan and evaluate his teaching and assessment methods.

If there is no set procedure, or you are not required to review your learners' progress, it would still be a useful activity if you have the time. The review process should be ongoing until your learner has completed their qualification, even if it is on an informal basis. Regular reviews can help to keep your learners motivated, make them feel less isolated, and appreciate how they are progressing so far. It is also an opportunity for your learners to contribute to the assessment process by voicing their views and discussing any concerns they may have.

The review process should involve:

- arranging a suitable date, time and location, and confirming these with your learner

- communicating with anyone else involved in the assessment process

- obtaining all relevant records relating to your learner, the subject and the assessments carried out

- discussing any issues or concerns, progress and achievements so far

- updating the assessment/action plan with achievements and dates

- identifying any training needs

- planning future assessment activities and target dates (ensuring these are SMART), along with the next review date

- signing and dating the review record and giving a copy to your learner.

Always listen to what your learners have to say, without interrupting them; they may not have the opportunity elsewhere to talk to someone about sensitive issues. Ensure the confidentiality of any information your learners disclose to you, otherwise you could lose their trust and respect. However, you need to know where your boundaries as an assessor stop, and not get involved personally. There are exceptions, i.e. if you have any cause for concern as to your learner's safety. For example, if you suspect bullying, then you must pass this information on to whoever is responsible in your organisation for safeguarding.

You could also review the progress of your learners as a group. At an appropriate time during the programme, you could hold a discussion regarding how they feel they are progressing. This is particularly useful when you need to assess group activities. It could be that some activities do not suit the learning styles of a few learners, therefore not enabling them to fully contribute. Using several different activities could alleviate this problem, and make the process more interesting. Feedback from group reviews can inform the assessment planning process, and also be a valuable tool to evaluate the programme as a whole.

When assessing and reviewing progress, always try to ensure that the environment meets your learners' basic needs, such as feeling safe and comfortable. This will enable them to feel secure enough to progress further. Maslow (1954) introduced the concept of a hierarchy of needs at different levels and this has been adapted by other theorists as time has progressed. The highest level is *self-actualising*, meaning people are fully functional, possess a healthy personality, and take responsibility for themselves and their actions. Maslow also believed that people should be able to move through these needs to the highest level, providing they are given an education that promotes growth.

Figure 3.1 shows the needs expressed as they might relate to learning.

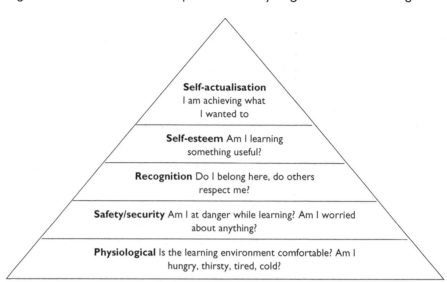

Figure 3.1: Maslow's (1954) hierarchy of needs expressed in educational terms

Ensuring the assessment environment meets your learners' physiological needs will enable them to feel comfortable and secure enough to learn and progress to the higher levels. You will need to appreciate that some learners may not have these lower needs met in their home lives, making it difficult for them to move on to the higher levels in their learning.

Supporting learners

At some point, you might have a learner who requires specialist support. Some learners will have needs, barriers or challenges that may affect their attendance and/or achievement. Hopefully, you can ascertain these prior to your learners commencing, perhaps from their application form or initial assessment. However, some needs may occur during the programme and you would need to plan a suitable course of action to help your learner, or refer them to an appropriate specialist or agency. If you can be proactive and notice potential needs before they become issues, you might be able to alleviate your learner's concerns. Otherwise, you will need to be reactive to the issue and deal with it professionally and sensitively.

Examples of potential needs, barriers and challenges might include:

- access to or fear of technology

- age

- culture and language differences

- emotional or psychological problems

- faith and religion

- finance

- hearing or visual impairment

- hyperactivity

- lack of confidence, motivation or social skills

- lack of resources

- learning difficulties and disabilities

- limited basic skills such as literacy, numeracy or information and communication technology (ICT)

- peer pressure

- personal/work/home circumstances

- physical, medical, mental or health problems.

When planning assessments, you need to consider any particular requirements of your learners, to ensure they can all participate. Initial assessment would ensure your learners are able to take the subject; however, you (or the organisation) may need to make reasonable adjustments to adapt resources, equipment or the environment to support them (as stated in the Equality Act 2010). If anything is adapted, make sure both you and your learners are familiar with the changes prior to carrying out the assessment activity. You cannot change the assessment criteria issued by the awarding organisation, but you can change the way you implement the assessment process. If you need to make any changes, you must consult the relevant awarding organisation to discuss these. Most will have an *Access to Assessment* policy which will inform you of what you can and cannot do. You cannot change a set examination date and time without approval, and you may need consent in writing for other changes or amendments to assessments.

Activity

Think about your learners and the environment in which you will be assessing. Do you need to ask your learners if any adaptations or changes are required? Will the timing of the assessments impact on your learners in any way, for example, during an evening session when they may not have had time to eat? Find out what you are allowed to amend in accordance with the qualification requirements. Check what documentation and guidance your awarding organisation provides to support learner needs.

You may feel you can deal with some of these yourself; however, you should always refer your learners to an appropriate specialist or agency if you can't deal with them. Never feel you have to solve any learner problems yourself and don't get personally involved; always remain professional.

All learners should have equality of opportunity and appropriate support to enable them to access assessment. It could be that you don't need to make any special arrangements just yet, but knowing what to do, and who to go to, will make things easier for you when such circumstances do occur.

Some learners may lack self-confidence, or have previous experiences of assessment that were not very positive. Many factors can affect your learners' motivation; therefore you need to ensure you treat all your learners as individuals, using their names, and making the assessment experience interesting and meaningful to them. Some learners may need more attention than others. Just because one learner is progressing well doesn't mean you can focus on those that aren't; all your learners need encouragement and feedback. You may not be able to change the environment or the resources you are using, but remaining professional and making the best use of what you have will help encourage your learners' development.

Example

Frank has a group of learners working towards a GCSE in geography. One of his learners, Rea, seems to be losing motivation and is not paying attention during sessions. As Frank knows she enjoys working with computers, he arranges for the class to move to the computer workshop to use a specialist website which has GCSE activities and online tests for learners to complete. These give immediate scores, which will help Frank monitor his learners' progress, and retain the motivation of Rea and the group.

You need to encourage your learners to reach their full potential. If you use assessment activities that are too difficult, learners may struggle and become frustrated and anxious. If assessments are too easy, learners may become bored. Knowing your learners and differentiating for their needs will enhance their motivation.

If you have learners who are quite motivated already, keep this motivation alive with regular challenges and constructive and positive feedback. A lack of motivation can lead to disruption and apathy. If you are teaching as well as assessing, ensure you are reaching all learning styles as everyone learns differently. Knowing what style your learners are will help you plan suitable assessment activities. You might not be able to change the formal assessments required, but you could devise informal assessments which will motivate and suit your learners' needs.

Example

Susan had always assessed her learners by assignments and tests. After encouraging them to take a learning styles test, she realised several of her learners prefer a kinaesthetic approach. She has therefore changed some of her informal assessments to include role play and practical activities to meet their learning styles.

Using the correct type of assessment to suit your learners, carrying out careful and appropriate assessment planning and reviewing progress will ensure you are meeting the needs of your learners. You will also make sure your learners are on the right pathway to achieving a successful result and that you are differentiating for any individual requirements.

Some learners may have barriers to assessment, for example, health problems or lack of access to a particular room or transport. You may also have to challenge your own values and beliefs if you don't agree with those of your learners to ensure you remain professional at all times. Other learners may have a support assistant who will be present during the assessment process. They will be there to help your learner in case they have any difficulties. Make sure you address your learner, not their assistant, to ensure you are including them fully in the process. If you have a learner with a speech impediment, give them time to finish speaking before continuing.

Your organisation should have support mechanisms to meet any special assessment requirements or individual needs of learners, for example, a learner services department.

Examples of support for learners:

- Dyspraxia – allow additional time and space if necessary for learners who have poor motor co-ordination.

- Dysgraphia – allow the use of a computer or other suitable media for learners who have difficulty with handwriting.

- Dyscalculia – allow additional time if necessary and use calculators or other equipment for learners who have difficulty with calculations or maths.

- Dyslexia – allow additional time or resources if necessary for learners who have difficulty processing language. Present written questions in a more simplified format, for example, bullet points. Ask questions verbally and make an audio or visual recording of your learner's responses; allow the use of a laptop for typing responses rather than expecting handwritten responses.

- A disability – learners could be assessed in a more comfortable environment where appropriate access and support systems are available. Learners could be given extra time to complete the assessment tasks, or to take medication privately. Dates could be rearranged to fit around doctor or hospital appointments.

- A hearing impairment – an induction loop could be used where all or part of an assessment is presented orally. Instructions and questions could be conveyed using sign language.

- A visual impairment – use large print or Braille, use specialist computer software if available, ask questions verbally and make an audio recording of your learner's responses.

- Varying work patterns – try to schedule the assessment at a time and place to suit.

- English as a second or other language – if allowed, try to arrange assessments in your learner's first language, for example, in Welsh. Many awarding organisations can translate assessment materials if requested. Bilingual assessments should also be offered.

Example

If you have a learner with dyslexia, it may be appropriate to ask questions rather than give a written test, or have someone to scribe their responses. For a learner who is partially sighted you could give papers in a larger font or use a magnified reading lamp. For a learner who is deaf, you could give a written test instead of an oral test. For a learner with Asperger's syndrome, you could use written questions rather than oral questions. For some learners who might struggle with spelling and grammar, the use of a computer could help. An adapted keyboard or a pen grip could help a learner with arthritis.

If you have a learner requiring support for any reason, there is a difference between *learning support* and *learner support*. Learning support relates to the subject, or help with language, literacy, numeracy or ICT skills. Learner support relates to any help your learner might need with personal issues, and/or general advice and guidance regarding their health, safety and welfare.

Always ask your learners how you can support them, but try to avoid making them feel different or uncomfortable. If you are unsure of what you can do to help your learners, ask your manager or internal quality assurer at your organisation. The Equality Act (2010) requires organisations to make reasonable adjustments where necessary. Don't assume you are on your own to carry out any amendment to provision; there should be specialist staff to help.

Extension Activity

Find out what is involved with the learner review process at your organisation. Is there a particular form you need to complete? Do you have to review all your learners regularly, for example, monthly or termly? How can you carry out informal reviews at times to suit both you and your learners?

A range of questioning techniques

Questions are a really useful type of formative assessment to ensure your learners are acquiring the necessary knowledge before moving on to a new topic. They can also be useful as a type of summative assessment at the end of a programme.

There are a variety of questioning techniques that you can use with groups or individuals. Questions can be oral (verbal) or written, for example, open questions requiring a full answer or closed questions requiring a yes or no answer. If you are asking questions verbally to a group of learners, ensure you include all learners. Don't just let the keen learners answer first as this gives the ones who don't know the answers the chance to stay quiet. Tell your learners you are going to use a particular method when you ask questions. For example, ask a question, pause for a second and then state the name of a learner who can answer. This way, all learners are thinking about the answer as soon as you have posed the question, and are ready to speak if their name is asked. This is sometimes referred to as pose, pause, pounce (PPP). If you use this process, make sure you have enough questions for everyone in the group so that no one is left out. If your nominated learner doesn't know the answer, ask them to guess. That way they still have to think and can't opt out. If they still don't know, say they made a good attempt and then move on to another learner for the answer.

To ensure you include everyone throughout your session, you could have a list of their names handy and tick each one off after you have asked them a question. This is fine if you don't have a large group. If you do, make sure you ask different learners each time you are in contact with them. When asking questions, only use one question in a sentence, as more than one may confuse your learners. Try not to ask *Does anyone have any questions?*, as often only those who are keen or confident will ask, and this doesn't tell you what your learners have learnt. Try not to use questions such as *Does that make sense?* or *Do you understand?*, as your learners will often say yes as they feel that's what you expect to hear.

Try to use open questions which require an answer to demonstrate knowledge and understanding. For example: *How many days are there in September?* This ensures your learner has to think about their answer. Using a closed question such as *Are there 30 days in September?* would only give a yes/no answer which doesn't show you if your learner has the required knowledge. Changing this to *How many days are there in September?* ensures your learner has to think about the answer and can't just guess. Open questions usually begin with who, what, when, where, why and how.

If you are having a conversation with your learner there are some other questioning techniques you can use. For example, you can ask probing questions to ascertain more information, which begin with: *Why was that?* You can prompt your learner to say more by asking *What about...?* You can clarify what your learner is saying by asking *Can you go over that again?* You can lead your learner by saying *So what you are saying is...* or you can ask a hypothetical question such as *What would you do if...?* It takes practice to use these techniques; however, they are a much better way of finding out information from your learners than asking a question that will only give a yes or no answer.

If there are no clear guidelines or assessment criteria for you to base your question on, you might find yourself being *subjective* rather than *objective*. That is, you make your own decision without any guidance and therefore base it on your opinion rather than fact. It is harder to remain objective when learners are responding to open questions which do not have clear assessment criteria or expected responses as a guide.

If you have to produce written questions for use with your learners, think how you will do this, i.e. short questions, essay-style questions with word counts, open, closed or multiple choice, etc. If you are giving grades, e.g. A, B, C, or pass/merit/distinction, you must have clear grading criteria to follow to make sure your decisions are objective, otherwise your learners may challenge your decisions.

Example

Haedish has a group of learners who need to achieve at least eight out of ten to achieve a pass. The questions have been written by a team of staff within the organisation, but no expected responses have been provided. Haedish has been told to use her professional judgement to make a decision, but finds this difficult. She knows her learners are very capable of achieving, but they don't always express themselves clearly when writing. She therefore devised a checklist to help her reach a decision. She also decided that any learner who achieves a lower mark will not be referred, but will be given the opportunity to respond verbally to the questions.

In this example, Haedish has made a decision to differentiate for her learners. However, she must first check with the other staff that this is acceptable, and if so, they must also be able to offer the same option to their learners. This will ensure that all assessors are being fair to all learners.

If you are writing multiple-choice questions, there should be a clear question and three or four possible answers. The question is known as the *stem*, the answer is called the *key* and the wrong answers are called *distractors*. Answers should always be similar in length and complexity (or use diagrams/pictures). Answers should not be confusing, and there should only be one definite key.

Example

Formative assessment is always:

(a) before the programme commences

(b) at the beginning of the programme

(c) ongoing throughout the programme

(d) when the programme ends.

You will see that all the answers contain a similar amount and type of words. None of the answers contains a clue from the question. A, B and D are the distractors and C is the correct answer (the key).

If you issue any assessment activities as homework, you need to plan your own time accordingly to ensure you are able to assess all the work that will be submitted on a certain date. It could be that your organisation expects you to assess and give feedback within a certain time period, for example, seven days.

If you are using the same questions for different learners at different times, be careful as they may pass the answers to each other. You may need to rephrase some questions if your learners are struggling with an answer as poor answers are often the result of poor questions. For essay and short-answer tests you should create sample answers to have something with which to compare. Be careful with the use of jargon – just because you understand it doesn't mean your learners will.

You need to be aware of learners colluding or plagiarising work, particularly now that so much information is available via the internet. Learners should take responsibility for referencing any sources in all work submitted, and may be required to sign an authenticity statement. If you suspect plagiarism, you could type a few of their words into an internet search engine or specialist program and see what appears. You would then have to challenge your learner as to whether it was intentional or not, and follow your organisation's plagiarism procedure.

Activity

Find out what your organisation's policy is regarding cheating, copying and plagiarism. Ensure all your learners are aware of it, and encourage them to sign and date all work submitted. This ensures they are taking ownership of their work.

Unfortunately, some learners do copy or plagiarise the work of others. Sometimes this is deliberate, and at other times it is due to a lack of knowledge of exactly what was required, or a misunderstanding when referencing quotes. If you feel the work that has been handed to you might not be the actual work of your learner, ask them some questions about it. This will confirm their knowledge, or otherwise. If you feel it isn't their work, you will need to confront them and let them know you will take the matter further. At this point your learner may confess or they may have what they consider a legitimate excuse. However, you must be certain the work is their own, otherwise it could be classed as fraud.

Example

Louise and Leanne are sisters, both taking a Certificate in Information Technology, which is assessed by assignments completed in their own time. When their assessor marked their work, he discovered the answers from both, which had been word-processed, were almost the same. He confronted them individually. Louise insisted the work was her own and had no idea why it looked similar to Leanne's. Leanne became quite upset and admitted to accessing Louise's files without her knowledge. She had been concerned at completing the work within the deadline. In this instance, the assessor credited Louise with the original work, and asked Leanne to re-do the assignment on her own.

It is easier to compare the work of your own learners; however, other assessors in your organisation might also assess the same programme with different learners. In this case, the internal quality assurer may pick up on issues when they are sampling learner work. It is difficult to check and compare the work of all learners, therefore the importance of authenticity must be stressed to everyone at the commencement of their programme and continually throughout. Asking learners to sign and date their work is always useful, particularly when it has been prepared on a computer.

Some ways of checking the authenticity of learners' work includes:

- syntax, spelling, grammar and punctuation – you know your learner speaks in a certain way at a certain level, yet their written work does not reflect this

- work that includes quotes which have not been referenced – without a reference source, this is direct plagiarism and could be a breach of copyright

- word-processed work that contains different fonts and sizes of text – this shows it could have been copied from the internet, or someone else's electronic file

- handwritten work that looks different to your learner's normal handwriting, or is not the same style or language as normally used, or word-processed work when they would normally write by hand

- work that refers to information you haven't taught, or is not relevant to the assessment criteria.

Electronic assessment systems often allow contact to take place between the learner and assessor through a website platform. You could communicate in this way, or via e-mail, and then compare the style of writing in the submitted work, to that within the communications.

The Copyright, Designs and Patents Act (1988) is the current UK copyright law. Copying the work of others without their permission would infringe the Act. Copyright is where an individual or organisation creates something as an original, and has the right to control the ways in which their work may be used by others. Normally the person who created the work will own the exclusive rights. However, if the work is produced as part of your employment, for example, if you produced several handouts or a workbook for your learners, then normally the work will belong to your organisation. Learners may be in breach of this Act if they plagiarise or copy the work of others without making reference to the original author.

Extension Activity

Design a questioning activity to carry out with your learners. This could be some oral questions that you will ask an individual learner or a multiple-choice test for a group of learners. Make sure you create expected responses. Use it with your learners and evaluate how effective it was. What would you change and why?

The role of ICT in assessment

Technology is constantly evolving and new resources are frequently becoming available. It's crucial to keep up to date with new developments and you should try to incorporate these within the assessment process. It's not only about you using technology to help assess your learners, but about your learners using it to complete their assessment activities. Encouraging your learners to use technology will help increase their skills in this area. Technology can be combined with traditional methods of assessment; for example, learners can complete a written assignment by word-processing their response and submitting it by e-mail or uploading it to a virtual learning environment (VLE). You can then give feedback via e-mail or the VLE system. Combining methods also promotes differentiation and inclusivity; for example, learners could access assessment materials via the VLE outside the normal learning environment to support their learning.

New and emerging technologies include using:

- blogs, chat rooms, social networking sites, webinars and online discussion forums to help learners communicate with each other
- computer facilities for learners to word-process their assignments and save documents and pictures
- digital media for visual/audio recording and playback
- electronic portfolios for learners to store their work
- e-mail for electronic submission of assessments, communication and informal feedback on progress
- interactive whiteboards for learners to use for presentations and to display their work
- internet access for research to support assignments or presentations
- mobile phones/smart phones for taking pictures, video and audio clips, and communicating
- networked systems to allow access to programs and documents from any computer linked to the system
- online and on-demand tests which can give instant results, for example, diagnostic, learning styles and multiple-choice tests
- online discussion forums which allow asynchronous (taking place at different times) and synchronous (taking place at the same time) discussions
- scanners for copying and transferring documents to a computer
- web cameras or video conferencing if you can't be in the same place as your learners and you need to observe a task
- VLEs to upload learning materials and assessment activities.

There will be advantages and limitations when using technology, see Table 3.6 overleaf.

Advantages	Limitations
<ul><li>auditable and reliable</li><li>accessible and inclusive</li><li>addressing sustainability, i.e. no need for paper copies</li><li>an efficient use of time and is cost-effective</li><li>give immediate results from online tests</li><li>accessible to learners, i.e. resources and materials at a time and place to suit</li><li>on demand, i.e. tests can be taken when a learner is ready</li></ul>	<ul><li>it can lead to plagiarism</li><li>it cannot be used during power cuts</li><li>finance is required to purchase new technology and computers</li><li>it might create barriers if learners cannot access or use technology</li><li>there might not be enough resources available for all learners to use at the same time</li><li>some learners might be afraid of using new technology</li><li>it is time consuming to set up initially</li></ul>

Table 3.6: Technology: advantages and limitations

If you are assessing the work of learners you might not have met, for example, by e-assessment, it can be very difficult to ensure the authenticity of their work. Your organisation might require each learner to attend an interview at some point and bring along some form of photo identification such as a driving licence, passport or employee card.

E-learning and assessment is constantly advancing. Unfortunately, there isn't room in this book to explain it in great detail, therefore please refer to other appropriate texts such as those listed at the end of this chapter.

Activity

Design an assessment activity that you could use with your learners, which incorporates ICT, for example an online quiz. If you have learners at the moment, use it with them and then evaluate how effective it was. What changes would you make and why?

Analysing learner achievement

If you have a group of learners whom you are testing, for example, using written questions to check their knowledge which might be graded, i.e. A–E, you will need to produce expected responses to ensure you are being fair when marking. If you don't you might find yourself subconsciously giving a higher mark to the best learners in your group. You should always remain objective when assessing, not have any favourite learners, and follow the marking criteria correctly. Otherwise, you may find your learners dispute your judgement and appeal against your decision. All learners have the right of appeal and there will be a procedure in your organisation for your learners to follow. It could be that another assessor reassesses your work to agree or disagree with your decision.

If you want to compare the achievements of your group against one another, you could use *norm-referencing*. This would proportion your marks accordingly, as there will always be those in your group who will achieve a high mark, and those who will achieve a low mark, leaving the rest in the middle. You would allocate your marks according to a quota, for example, the top 20 per cent would achieve an A, the next 20 per cent a B, and so on. Norm-referencing uses the achievement of a group to set the standards for specific grades, or for how many learners will pass or fail. This type of assessment is useful to maintain consistency of results over time; whether the test questions are easy or hard, there will always be those achieving a high grade or a lower grade, whatever their marks.

Example

Petra has a group of 25 learners who have just taken a test consisting of 20 questions – she wants to allocate grades A–E to her group. She has worked out the top 20 per cent will achieve an A, the second 20 per cent a B and so on. When she marks the tests, she is surprised to see the lowest mark was 16 out of 20, meaning a grade E. Even though the learners had done well in the test, they were still given a low grade in comparison to the rest of the group.

A fairer method of marking would have been to set a pass mark, for example, 15 out of 20. Learners achieving 14 or below could retake a different test at a later date.

Criterion-referencing enables learners to achieve based upon their own merit, as their achievements are not compared with one another. All learners therefore have equality of opportunity. If grades are allocated, for example, a distinction, credit or pass, there will be specific criteria which must have been met for each. These criteria will be supplied by the awarding organisation, or you may need to produce them yourself.

Example

Pass – described the activity.

Credit – described and analysed the activity.

Distinction – described, analysed and critically reflected upon the activity.

Some qualifications may simply be achieved by a pass or a fail, for example, a multiple-choice test where learners must achieve seven out of ten for a pass. You would have a list of the correct responses, thus enabling you to mark objectively. You will also have regulations to follow in the event of a fail as to whether your learner can retake the test, and if so, when. Online testing often utilises multiple-choice questions, and instant results can be given. This is fine for summative assessments, however, it might not be a good idea to use language such as pass or fail for formative assessments. Formative assessments are designed to aid development and negative results could demoralise your learners. However, you could always use terms such as pass or refer: any learners with a refer result could have the opportunity to retake the same test, or an alternative one, at a later date.

If learners are retaking the same test, it's advisable to leave a period of time, for example, seven days, before they take it again. If learners are taking a test that other learners have already attempted, you need to ensure they have not communicated their responses. If learners feel the urge to cheat, they are ultimately only cheating themselves. A bank of questions would be useful; this way you could choose a certain number of random questions that will always be different. Computer-generated question papers should automatically choose different questions for different learners. If you are giving any guidance to learners who have been referred, for example, their assignment needs more work, make sure you don't give too much support to the extent that their response is based on your guidance, not their own knowledge.

Sometimes, negative marking is used whereby a mark is deducted for every incorrect answer.

If you assess a programme which requires grades to be given to learners, you will need to analyse the data regarding their achievements. The grades could be expressed as:

- 1, 2, 3, 4, 5
- A, B, C, D, E

- Achieved/not achieved
- competent/not yet competent
- distinction, credit, pass, fail
- pass, refer, fail
- percentages, e.g. 80 per cent
- satisfactory, good, outstanding.

Analysing the results will help you see not only how well your learners have done, but whether there are any trends. For example, if all your learners received an average of C, but another assessor's group achieved an average of B, is there a fault on your part?

If you had a group of 30 learners who all achieved an A grade, was this due to your excellent teaching, the skills and knowledge of your learners, or by being too lenient with your grades when marking?

If you had a group of 15 learners who all failed an assignment, you could ask yourself the same questions. However, it could be that the assignment questions were worded in a confusing way, or you had given the assignment too early in the programme. If most of your group averaged a grade of 50 per cent, whereas a colleague's group averaged 80 per cent, was this because you had given your learners misleading or ambiguous information relating to that topic?

Asking yourself these questions will help you ascertain if you are producing assessments that are fit for purpose, and if not, you will need to do something about it. For example, you may need to amend your teaching or assessment methods, reword your questions or redesign some assessment activities.

Making decisions and giving feedback

You may find, when assessing, that your learners haven't achieved everything they should have. When making a decision, you need to base this on all the information or evidence available to you at the time. If your learner has not met all the assessment criteria, you need to give constructive feedback, discuss any inconsistencies and give advice on what they should do next. If your learner disagrees with your decision, they are entitled to follow the appeals procedure. If you are having difficulty making a decision, discuss this with your manager or a colleague to obtain a second opinion. You need to be fully confident when making decisions. Never feel under pressure to pass learners who have not fully achieved, for example, due to targets or funding. You are not doing yourself or your learners any favours by saying they have achieved something when they haven't.

Feedback can be informal and given during a teaching session, a one-to-one review or by telephone, e-mail or another relevant method. Verbal feedback could be given when you next see your learner, or if there are time constraints you might just give them back their work with the feedback attached for them to read later. It is always good practice to point out any errors in spelling, grammar, punctuation and syntax to help your learners realise their mistakes. Always give your learner a copy and keep the original yourself for audit purposes. Encourage your learners to get in touch if they need to clarify any points in your feedback.

Feedback should be formalised by using an assessment document such as the *performance and knowledge record* opposite. The form could be word-processed each time an aspect is assessed, allowing it to be added to over time.

When giving feedback, you should always try to be constructive (to help retain your learner's motivation), specific (by stating exactly what was achieved) and developmental (by encouraging further learning, e.g. reading and research) with what you say. You also need to make sure you are not being ambiguous or vague, therefore leaving your learner not really knowing what they have achieved. You need to be factual regarding what they have achieved in relation to the assessment criteria, and not just give your opinion. It is important to keep your learners motivated, and what you say can help or hinder their progress and confidence.

Example

All Fatima's learners had passed the required assessment criteria for their first assignment. When marking these, Fatima just wrote 'pass', along with 'good' on each piece of work. Although there were a few spelling and grammatical errors within them all, she did not correct any. She didn't have time to make any comments about how each learner could develop.

See Chapter 2 for more details regarding assessment decisions, how to give feedback and record keeping.

Example

Performance and knowledge record	
Learner: Marcia Indira	Assessor: Abbi Cross
Qualification and level: Level 2 Business, Administration and Finance	
Unit 1: Business Enterprise	Learning outcome 2: Be able to develop a business enterprise idea
Date assessed: 21 October 2011	Date feedback given: 25 October 2011

Aspects assessed	Feedback
Q1 – Generate a range of ideas for a business enterprise	I like the ideas you have generated for your business; you have come up with some very original concepts. I feel your idea could become a real business opportunity. Do be careful when you are word-processing your work as you have a few spelling errors. For example, *where* for *were* and *been for being*. If you were putting a proposal together to talk to investors you must ensure it is correct and professional. You could consider looking at various enterprise websites and Business Link.
Q2 – Compare the viability of the business enterprise ideas	You have looked at the viability of your business by researching what is available elsewhere, and compared your ideas to them. I like the way you have presented this task using graphs and tables. You do seem to have a really good idea that would benefit a lot of people. I would recommend you use some colour rather than black and white to make your points stand out.
Q3 – Select and develop a business idea	You selected your idea as proposed in Q1 and have now followed your ideas through to the development of a business plan. Your plan is very professional looking and has taken into consideration everything we have discussed during the sessions. I enjoyed watching your presentation to your peers regarding your idea and how it will progress to the investment stage. Peer feedback was positive and your own self-evaluation was fair and objective.
	You have now successfully achieved learning outcome 2 – well done! We will create a separate action plan for the next learning outcome.
Assessment was conducted under the specified conditions or context	
Assessment decision:	valid ✓ authentic ✓ current ✓ sufficient ✓ reliable ✓
	Achieved? **YES**/NO
	Action required? YES/**NO**
	Feedback and action record completed? YES/NO **N/A**
Signed assessor: *A Cross*	Signed learner: *Marcia Indira*
Countersignature and date (if required):	

Table 3.7: Performance and knowledge record

While the learners in the example were probably happy they had achieved a pass, they would not be aware of what they could improve upon, what was good about their work, or that they had made some mistakes. They would therefore continue to make these mistakes, as they would not know any different. It could be that Fatima didn't even spot the mistakes herself. However, you would not want to demoralise your learners by writing too much for their first assessment activity; a combination of written and oral feedback might be better to retain motivation.

Evaluating the programme

You should evaluate the full assessment process for each programme or qualification you assess. You could evaluate the resources you used, for example, handouts, to ensure they are inclusive, promote equality and engage with diversity. There might have been some equipment which was faulty and will need to be fixed or changed. You could evaluate whether the assessment types and methods you used were successful or if there were any trends which need addressing. You will need to ensure the activities you used to assess skills, knowledge and understanding were valid and reliable, and that you only assessed the criteria you were meant to assess. You will need to ask yourself if you assessed fairly and ethically, or if you had a favourite learner to whom you gave more attention, or were lenient with for any reason.

You could use questionnaires to gain feedback from learners and others, which will help you evaluate your programme. See Chapter 4 for information regarding surveys and questionnaires.

Extension Activity

Evaluate a recent assessment activity you have carried out with your learners. Did you need to differentiate it in any way? Were there any trends with the results and, if so, what will you do now?

Continuing professional development

Continuing professional development (CPD) should be carried out regularly, to maintain your occupational competence not only as an assessor but also regarding your subject and any developments in new technology.

As a professional, you need to continually update your skills and knowledge. This knowledge relates not only to your subject specialism, but assessment methods, the types of learners you will be assessing, and relevant internal and external requirements. CPD can be formal or informal, planned well in advance or be opportunistic, but it should have a real impact upon your job role and lead to an improvement in your practice. CPD is more than just attending events; it is also using critical reflection regarding your experiences which results In your development as an assessor. Shadowing colleagues, observing how they assess, joining professional associations, and internet research regarding your subject will all help your development.

Opportunities for CPD include:

- attending events, meetings, standardisation activities and training programmes
- e-learning activities
- evaluating feedback from peers and learners
- improving skills such as language, literacy, numeracy and ICT
- membership of professional associations or committees
- observing and shadowing colleagues
- researching developments or changes to your subject and/or relevant legislation
- self-reflection
- studying for relevant qualifications
- subscribing to and reading relevant journals and websites
- visiting other organisations
- voluntary work
- work experience placements
- writing or reviewing books and articles.

You will need to maintain a record of all CPD undertaken to prove you are remaining current with your assessment role and subject specialism. If it's a requirement for your job role, you may need to register with the Institute for Learning (IfL). They will require you to carry out a certain number of hours per year of CPD and they can ask to see your records. You could keep a manual record such as the one shown in Table 3.8 on page 122, an electronic record, or upload your details to IfL's own CPD website called *Reflect*. Using a reference number for each activity enables you to cross-reference the activities to the evidence, for example, number 1 could be minutes of meetings, number 2 could be a certificate, number 3 a record of achievement, etc. It also enables you to locate them when necessary. Besides keeping this record up to date, you should write a more detailed reflection of what you learnt and how it impacted upon your job role.

Example

Continuing professional development record					
Name: *Abbi Cross*		Organisation: *Excellence Training College*		IfL number: *AA002233*	
Date	Activity and venue	Duration	Justification towards assessment role and subject specialism	Further training needs	Ref. no.
06 Jan 2012	Attendance at college standardisation event. Four assessors, myself and the IQA discussed how we interpreted the requirements of units 101, 102 and 103 and re-assessed each other's decisions.	3 hrs	Standardised assessment practice to ensure I am assessing the Level 3 Certificate in Hospitality & Catering in the same way as the other assessors.	Units 104 and 105 to be looked at next time.	1
10 Feb 2012	Attendance at a First Aid training day.	6 hrs	To ensure I am current with First Aid in case someone has an accident.	–	2
20 Mar 2012	Attendance at staff training event for assessors at college. All assessors were able to get together and discuss the types of records we use. We were also given updates regarding college's policies and procedures.	3 hrs	Ensured I am up to date with college procedures regarding assessment practice.	–	3

Table 3.8: CPD record

You can update your CPD record at any time. However, if you are registered with the IfL, you will need to declare your CPD annually and they will e-mail you a reminder.

You will probably participate in an appraisal or performance review system at your organisation. This is a valuable opportunity to discuss your learning, development and any training or support you may need in the future. It is also a chance to reflect upon your achievements and successes. Always keep a copy of any documentation relating to your training and CPD, as you may need to provide this to funding bodies, awarding organisations or regulatory bodies if requested.

Having the support of your organisation will help you decide what is relevant to your development as an assessor, and your job role.

The practice of assessment has been recognised as a professional activity by the granting of Chartered Status to the Institute of Educational Assessors (CIEA). Their aim is to improve the quality of assessment in schools and colleges by working with educational assessors to develop their knowledge, understanding and capability in all aspects of educational testing and assessment. You can access their standards by visiting their website (www.ciea.org.uk).

Reflecting upon your own assessment practice, taking account of feedback from learners and colleagues, evaluating your practice and maintaining your professional development will enable you to become a more effective assessor.

Extension Activity

Decide on a method for documenting your CPD. You could use a form as in Table 3.8, or you could design your own. Reflect upon each CPD event and how it will impact upon your role as an assessor. If you haven't already done so, join the IfL (www.ifl.ac.uk) and have a go at using their Reflect CPD program.

Summary

In this chapter you have learnt about:

- assessment planning in other contexts
- managing and reviewing the assessment process
- a range of questioning techniques
- the role of ICT in assessment
- CPD.

Evidence from the completed activities, plus the following, could be used towards the *Assessing vocational skills, knowledge and understanding* unit, for example:

- four completed assessment/action plans with at least two learners (methods must include those used to assess skills, knowledge and understanding in an environment which is not a learner's place of work)

- four assessment activities you would use with your learners (e.g. assignment, case study, multiple choice test, written questions)

- four completed feedback records for the two learners

- schemes of work and session plans showing assessment activities

- minutes of assessor team meetings

- records of standardisation activities

- written statements cross-referenced to the TAQA unit's assessment criteria

- answers to questions issued by the awarding organisation

- records of discussions with your assessor

Cross-referencing grid

This chapter contributes towards the following three TAQA units' assessment criteria. Full details of the learning outcomes and assessment criteria for each TAQA unit can be found in the Appendices.

TAQA unit	Assessment criteria
Understanding the principles and practices of assessment	2.1 3.1, 3.2 4.2, 4.3, 4.4 6.3 7.2 8.2, 8.3, 8.4
Assess occupational competence in the work environment	1.1 2.1 3.1, 3.2, 3.3 4.2, 4.3, 4.4
Assess vocational skills, knowledge and understanding	1.1, 1.2, 1.3 2.1, 2.2, 2.3, 2.4, 2.5, 2.6 3.1, 3.2, 3.3 4.1, 4.2, 4.3, 4.4

Theory focus

References and further information

Belbin, M (1993) *Team Roles At Work*. Oxford: Elsevier Science and Technology.

Berne, E (1973) *Games People Play: The Psychology of Human Relationships*. London: Penguin Books.

Bloom, BS (1956) *Taxonomy of Educational Objectives: The Classification of Educational Goals*. New York: McKay.

Boud, D (1995) *Enhancing Learning Through Self-assessment*. London: Kogan Page.

Gravells, A (2012) *Preparing to Teach in the Lifelong Learning Sector*. Exeter: Learning Matters.

Hill, C (2008) *Teaching with E-learning in the Lifelong Learning Sector* (2nd edition). Exeter: Learning Matters.

JISC (2010) *Effective Assessment in a Digital Age: A guide to Technology-enhanced Assessment and Feedback*. Bristol: JISC Innovation Group. Available at: www.jisc.ac.uk/digiassess.

Maslow, AH (1987) *Motivation and Personality* (3rd revised edition; ed. Frager, R). New York: Pearson Education.

Murphy, P (1999) *Learners, Learning and Assessment*. London: Paul Chapman Publishing.

Ofqual (2009) *Authenticity – a guide for teachers*. Coventry: Ofqual.

Pachler, N et al. (2009) *Scoping a Vision for Formative E-assessment* (FEASST). JISC.

Reece, I and Walker, S (2007) *Teaching, Training and Learning: A Practical Guide* (6th edition). Sunderland: Business Education Publishers.

Tummons, J (2011) *Assessing Learning in the Lifelong Learning Sector* (3rd edition). Exeter: Learning Matters.

Websites

Association for Achievement and Improvement through Assessment (AAIA): www.aaia.org.uk

Belbin team role descriptors: www.belbin.com/content/page/49/BELBIN%20Team%20Role%20Summary%20Descriptions.pdf

Berne transactional analysis theory: www.ericberne.com/transactional_analysis_description.htm

Chartered Institute of Educational Assessors: www.ciea.org.uk

Copyright, Designs and Patents Act (1988): www.legislation.gov.uk/ukpga/1988/48/contents

Equality Act (2010): www.legislation.gov.uk/ukpga/2010/15/contents

Institute for Learning: www.ifl.ac.uk

Maslow: www.maslow.com

Oxford Learning Institute: Giving and receiving feedback: www.learning.ox.ac.uk/supervision/stages/feedback/

Peer and self-assessment: www.nclrc.org/essentials/assessing/peereval.htm

Plagiarism: www.plagiarism.org and www.plagiarismadvice.org

Post-compulsory education and training: www.pcet.net

QCF shortcut: http://tinyurl.com/2944r8h

Support for adult learners: www.direct.gov.uk/adultlearning

CHAPTER 4
PRINCIPLES AND PRACTICES OF INTERNALLY ASSURING THE QUALITY OF ASSESSMENT

Introduction

In this chapter you will learn about:

- key concepts and principles of internal quality assurance (IQA)
- roles and responsibilities of an internal quality assurer (IQA)
- sample planning and the collection of information
- maintaining and improving the quality of assessment
- evaluation

There are activities and examples which will help you reflect on the above and will assist your knowledge of the principles and practices of internally assuring the quality of assessment. Completing the activities will help you to gather evidence towards the TAQA *Principles and practices of internally assuring the quality of assessment* unit. At the end of each section is an extension activity to stretch and challenge your learning further.

At the end of the chapter is a list of possible evidence which could be used towards the TAQA *Principles and practices of internally assuring the quality of assessment* unit.

A cross-referencing grid shows how the content of this chapter contributes towards the three TAQA units' internal quality assurance criteria. There is also a theory focus with relevant references, further information and websites to which you might like to refer.

Key concepts and principles of internal quality assurance (IQA)

Quality *assurance* can be defined as a system to monitor and evaluate a product or a service. It should identify and recommend measures to make improvements to standards and performance or at least maintain the status quo if everything is working well. To the contrary, quality *control* seeks to find problems whereas quality assurance seeks to avoid problems, stabilise, and improve products and services.

Internal quality assurance (IQA) relates to the monitoring of the learner journey throughout their time with you. It also includes monitoring the training and assessment activities, which are a substantial part of the IQA process. Internal verification was the previous term used for monitoring assessment, however, IQA monitors the whole process from when a learner commences to when they leave.

The IQA process relates to a product, i.e. a learner taking a qualification which is accredited by an awarding organisation. It can also relate to a service to develop people, for example, to help staff perform their job roles better or work towards a promotion. If you are internally quality assuring an accredited qualification, there should be an external quality assurer (EQA) from the awarding organisation who will monitor your practice. You will need to find out who this is and maintain regular contact with them. At some point they will sample the assessment and IQA systems. See Chapter 5 (page 181) for more information regarding the EQA process.

IQA rationale

A good IQA system will start with a written rationale; this is the reason *why* IQA should take place. This could be due to the qualification being accredited and the requirements for assessors and IQAs to hold a recognised qualification (whether the assessment strategy for the subject requires it or not).

Example

The IQA rationale is to comply with internal and external organisations' requirements to assure the quality of assessment for all learners. All assessment decisions will be carried out by qualified assessors in each subject area and sampled by qualified IQAs. This will ensure the safety, fairness, validity and reliability of assessment methods and decisions. It will also uphold the credibility of the qualification and reputation of the organisation.

Having a rationale will help ensure assessment and IQA activities are robust, and that they are safe, valid, fair and reliable.

- Safe: e.g. the methods used are ethical, there is little chance of plagiarism, the work can be confirmed as authentic, confidentiality is taken into account, learning and assessment is not compromised, nor is the learner's experience or potential to achieve (safe in this context does not relate to health and safety but to the methods used).

- Valid: e.g. the methods used are based on the requirements of the qualification or job specification.

- Fair: e.g. the methods used are appropriate to all learners at the required level, taking into account any particular learner needs.

- Reliable: e.g. a similar decision would be made with similar learners.

IQA process

Quality assurance should be carried out from commencement to the completion of the product or service. If there is no external formal examination taken by learners, there has to be a system of monitoring the performance of assessors. If not, assessors might make incorrect judgements or pass someone who hasn't met the requirements perhaps because they were biased towards them. Assessment and IQA systems should be monitored and evaluated continuously to identify any actions for improvement, which should then be implemented. This also includes the continuing professional development (CPD) of assessors and IQAs.

An IQA must be appointed to carry out the quality role within an organisation where there are assessment activities taking place.

As a minimum, the IQA should:

- plan what will be monitored, from whom and when

- observe assessor practice and give developmental feedback

- sample assessment records, learners' work and assessor decisions

- meet with learners and others, for example, witnesses

- facilitate the standardisation of assessor practice

- support assessors

If there is more than one IQA for a particular subject area, one person should take the lead role and co-ordinate the others. Please see Chapter 6 for further details. All IQAs should standardise their practice with each other to ensure they interpret the requirements in the same way.

If IQA does not take place, there are risks to the accuracy, consistency and fairness of assessment practice. This could lead to incorrect decisions and ultimately disadvantage the learners.

Depending upon the subject you will IQA, you will usually follow the IQA cycle. The cycle will continue to ensure the assessment process is constantly monitored and improved. Records of all activities must be maintained throughout to satisfy your organisation, the regulatory authorities and awarding organisations.

Figure 4.1: Internal quality assurance (IQA) cycle

The cycle involves the following steps.

- Identify the product or service – ascertain what is to be assessed and quality assured and why. For example, are learners working towards a qualification or are staff being observed performing their job roles? The criteria will need to be clear, i.e. units from a qualification or aspects of a job specification. Learners should be allocated to assessors in a fair way, for example, according to location or workload.

- Planning – devise a sample plan to arrange what will be monitored, from whom and when. Plan the dates to observe assessor practice and hold team meetings and standardisation activities. Information will need to be obtained from assessors to assist the planning process and risks taken into account such as assessor knowledge and experience.

- Activity – carry out the IQA activities such as sampling learners' work, observing assessor practice and sampling assessor records and decisions. It also includes holding meetings and standardisation activities, supporting and training assessors and communicating with others involved in the assessment and IQA process.

- Decision and feedback – make a judgement as to whether the assessor has performed satisfactorily and made valid and reliable decisions. Give developmental feedback as to what was good or what could be improved. Agree action points if necessary and follow them up. See Chapter 5 for further information regarding giving feedback to assessors.

- Evaluation – review the whole process of assessment and IQA to determine what could be improved. Agree action plans if necessary; implement and follow them up. Follow any action plans from EQAs or others involved in the IQA process. Write self-assessment reports.

The cycle will then begin again with an identification of what needs to be monitored and when. Throughout the cycle, standardisation of practice between IQAs should take place; this will help ensure the consistency and fairness of decisions. Records must be maintained of all IQA activities. All staff should maintain their CPD and follow legal and organisational requirements. If the qualification is accredited by an awarding organisation, EQA will also take place to ensure IQA is effective.

Activity

Obtain a copy of the qualification handbook or other criteria that will be assessed and internally quality assured. Familiarise yourself with the IQA requirements and decide what aspects of the assessment process you will monitor and why.

Concepts of internal quality assurance

Concepts are the aspects involved throughout the IQA process. They include:

- accountability
- achievement
- assessment strategies
- confidentiality
- risk factors

- evaluation

- interim or summative sampling

- transparency

You need to be *accountable* to your organisation to ensure you are carrying out your role as an IQA correctly. Your assessors should know why they are being monitored and why their decisions are being sampled. You will also be accountable to the awarding organisation if you assess an accredited programme. For example, if you or an assessor does something wrong the credibility of your reputation could be questioned.

You may be required to analyse *achievement* data and compare this to national or organisational targets. The funding your organisation receives might also be related to achievements. It's always a useful evaluation method to keep a record of how many learners your assessors have and how many successfully achieve. If one assessor has a high number of learners who leave, is it because of the assessor or some other factor?

Following the *assessment strategy* for your subject will ensure you are carrying out your IQA role correctly, are holding or working towards the required IQA qualifications and are supporting your assessors. You might also need to recruit and interview new assessors if more are needed and ensure they meet the assessment strategy (if applicable). Conversely, you will need to have succession planning arrangements in place if an assessor leaves at short notice. You can't have learners left without an assessor.

Confidentiality will ensure you maintain records in accordance with organisational and statutory guidelines such as the Data Protection Act (2003) and Freedom of Information Act (2000).

There are many *risk factors* to take into consideration when planning IQA activities. For example:

- assessor expertise, confidence and competence, whether new, experienced, qualified or working towards an Assessor Award

- assessors (or teachers/trainers) who assess the same subject but with different groups of learners

- whether the learners have been registered with an awarding organisation (if applicable)

- workload and case load of assessors

- locations of learners and assessors

- type of qualification or programme being assessed, problem areas or units

- changes to standards and qualifications

- assessment methods and types of evidence provided by learners

- whether evidence and records are manual or electronic

- reliability of witnesses

- authenticity of learners' work

All the above can impact upon the amount of IQA activities which need to be carried out, with whom and when.

Evaluation of the assessment and IQA process should always take place to inform current and future practice. All aspects of the IQA cycle should be evaluated on a continuous basis.

Sampling should also take place on an ongoing basis and not be left until the end of the programme. It should be *interim*, i.e. part way through and *summative*, i.e. at the completion stage. If a problem is identified at the interim stage, there is a chance to put it right. The summative stage can check the full assessment process has been successfully completed and that all documents are signed and dated correctly.

To assist *transparency*, you need to ensure that everyone who is involved in the assessment and IQA process clearly understands what is expected and can see there is nothing untoward taking place. That includes your own interpretation and understanding of the assessment criteria as well as that of your assessors. There should be no ambiguity, i.e. everyone should know what is expected of them. Auditable records must always be maintained throughout the IQA process. If your organisation is claiming funding, full and accurate records must be maintained to show what was claimed and why.

Principles of internal quality assurance

Principles are functions which are based upon the concepts, for example, *how* the IQA process is put into practice.

One important principle is known as VACSR and applies to assessment as well as internal quality assurance. You need to ensure all assessed work is:

- **V**alid – the work is relevant to the assessment criteria.

- **A**uthentic – the work has been produced solely by the learner.

- **C**urrent – the work is still relevant at the time of assessment.

- **S**ufficient – the work covers all the assessment criteria.

- **R**eliable – the work is consistent across all learners, over time and at the required level.

If the above is not checked, you will not be supporting your assessors correctly. This could lead them to think their practice is acceptable when in reality it might not be.

Key principles of internal quality assurance include:

- assessor competence – ensuring assessors are experienced and competent at their role, meeting the requirements of the assessment strategy (if applicable) and are maintaining their CPD

- communication – ensuring this takes place regularly with learners, assessors, other IQAs, employers, witnesses, etc.

- CPD – maintaining currency of knowledge and performance to ensure your IQA practice is up to date

- equality and diversity – ensuring all assessment activities embrace equality, inclusivity and diversity, represent all aspects of society and meet the requirements of the Equality Act 2010 (see Chapter 1 (page 23) for further details)

- ethics – ensuring the assessment and IQA process is honest and moral, and takes into account confidentiality and integrity

- fairness – ensuring assessment and IQA activities are fit for purpose, and planning, decisions and feedback are justifiable

- health and safety – ensuring these are taken into account throughout the full assessment and IQA process, carrying out risk assessments as necessary

- motivation – encouraging and supporting your assessors to reach their maximum potential

- record keeping – ensuring accurate records are maintained throughout the learning, assessment and IQA process

- SMART – ensuring all assessment activities are **s**pecific, **m**easurable, **a**chievable, **r**ealistic and **t**ime bound

- standardisation – ensuring the assessment and IQA requirements are interpreted accurately and that all assessors and IQAs are making comparable and consistent decisions

- strategies – ensuring a written strategy is in place which clearly explains the full process of what will be internally quality assured, when and how.

Following the concepts and principles of internal quality assurance will ensure you are performing your role as an IQA according to all relevant regulations and requirements

Extension Activity

Look at the bulleted lists of concepts and principles and describe how each will impact upon your role as an IQA. You may need to research some aspects further or speak to relevant staff at your organisation.

Roles and responsibilities of an IQA

Usually, IQAs are also experienced assessors in the subject area they are quality assuring. For example, if the subject area is motor vehicle maintenance, they should not be able to quality assure hairdressing. The IQA process might be the same for each subject, but the IQA must be fully familiar with the assessment criteria to give a valid and reliable decision. If you have not already read the preceding chapters regarding assessment, you will find them useful to update your assessment knowledge. If you are quality assuring an accredited qualification, you will need to read the assessment strategy from the awarding organisation to see if it states that you must also be a qualified assessor in the same subject that you will IQA.

Your main role will be to carry out the IQA process according to the qualification requirements, or those of the programme or job specification which is being assessed. Your roles and responsibilities will include far more than those stated in the IQA cycle in Figure 4.1 on page 130. However, there might be a quality assurance manager in your organisation who will be responsible for some of the duties.

Your role might include:

- advising, supporting and providing developmental feedback to assessors
- documenting the quality assurance strategy, process and decisions

- ensuring assessors interpret, understand and consistently apply the correct standards and requirements

- identifying issues and trends

- interviewing learners, assessors and other relevant staff

- leading standardisation activities to ensure the accuracy and consistency of assessment decisions between assessors

- monitoring and observing the full learner journey from commencement to completion

- planning and carrying out sampling of assessed work

- taking part in CPD

- working towards relevant IQA qualifications

The IQA unit is at level 4 on the Qualifications and Credit Framework (QCF), whereas the Assessor unit is at level 3. This demonstrates the importance of the IQA role. Often IQAs are supervisors or managers and are naturally responsible for staff, systems and procedures. Some IQAs are still working as assessors and performing both roles. That's absolutely fine as long as they do not IQA their own assessment decisions as that would be a conflict of interest. Some smaller organisations might only have one assessor and one IQA, which again is fine providing the IQA remains fully objective when carrying out their role. Some small teams, i.e. one assessor and one IQA, can swap roles and IQA each other's assessment decisions. Again, it's not a problem unless the organisation deems it is. It could be considered a good way of standardising practice as they will be monitoring each other regularly to ensure consistency.

Activity

Have a look at the TAQA standards in Appendices 4 and 5. Look at the learning outcomes and assessment criteria to see what an internal quality assurer should know and do. Appendix 4 relates to knowledge and Appendix 5 to performance.

IQAs might also be required to:

- analyse enrolment, retention, achievement and success figures

- carry out a training needs analysis with assessors

- compile self-assessment reports

- countersign other IQAs' judgements

- deal with appeals and complaints

- design advertising and marketing materials

- ensure qualifications are fit for purpose and validated by the organisation

- ensure strategies, policies and procedures are regularly reviewed

- facilitate appropriate staff development, training and CPD

- induct and mentor new staff, support existing staff and carry out appraisals

- interview new staff

- liaise with others involved in the IQA process, e.g. trainers, witnesses and external quality assurers

- monitor questionnaires and surveys and set action plans

- prepare agendas and chair meetings

- prepare for external inspections and awarding organisation visits and implement any action points

- provide statistics and reports to line managers

- register and certificate learners with an awarding organisation

- set targets and/or performance indicators

You should always follow any organisational and regulatory requirements such as the *Regulatory Arrangements for the Qualifications and Credit Framework* (2008) for England, Wales and Northern Ireland.

> *The qualifications regulators will therefore use these arrangements in protecting the interests of learners and promoting public confidence in the national qualifications system. The regulatory arrangements are designed to reflect the qualifications regulators' policy commitment to a strategic, risk-based approach to safeguarding the interests of learners.*
>
> (Ofqual, 2008, p3)

The term National Vocational Qualifications (NVQs), which relate to qualifications predominantly assessed in the work environment, will be changing due to the QCF. However, the NVQ Code of Practice (2006) will still apply if you are involved with them prior to the change.

There will be other requirements you need to follow such as those imposed by the awarding organisation if you are quality assuring an accredited qualification. There will also be subject-specific guidance and legislation such as the Health and Safety at Work etc. Act (1974), and the Equality Act (2010). See Chapter 1 for further details.

Extension Activity

Find out what documents you need to use to support the IQA process at your organisation. Are they available in hard copy format, or can you access and use them electronically? Will you have to design your own? Explain how each document relates to the various functions of the IQA cycle.

Sample planning and the collection of information

To perform your IQA role fully, you need to create sample plans, monitor activities and collect information. You might have several plans for different activities, for example, a plan to observe your assessors, a plan to sample their assessed work, and a plan for meetings and standardisation activities. You might be able to combine the plans if there are only a small number of assessors. To help you plan effectively, you need to have an IQA strategy on which to base your activities.

IQA strategy

Think of the IQA strategy as the starting point for all the activities, monitoring and sampling which you will carry out. It should be a written statement of what will be carried out and is based on the IQA rationale and any identified risk factors. Having a strategy will help you plan what will be monitored and ensure that your quality assurance systems are fit for purpose. If you are quality assuring an accredited qualification, it will be a requirement of the awarding organisation that you have a written strategy.

Systems should be in place to ensure all concepts and principles are met and that monitoring and sampling is effective. The strategy might be produced by your organisation or it might be your responsibility to write it.

Example

IQA strategy for Level 2 Customer Service (one IQA, four assessors, 100 learners).

The IQA will:

- *observe each assessor every six months*
- *talk to a sample of learners and witnesses*
- *sample at least five assessed units from each assessor across a mix of learners (new assessors will have a higher sample rate)*
- *chair a monthly team meeting*
- *facilitate a bi-monthly standardisation activity to cover all units over a period of time*
- *maintain full records of all IQA activities*
- *implement external quality assurance action points.*

The IQA strategy should take into account factors such as:

- assessment methods (are they safe, valid, fair and reliable; are they complex and varied; do they include online assessments; are witnesses used?)

- availability of assessors for observations and meetings (some assessors could be located at a distance, can activities take place remotely via the internet?)

- experience, workload and caseload of assessors (experienced assessors can be sampled less than new assessors; some assessors might work part time or have other work commitments; some assessors might have more learners than others)

- holistic assessment (if more than one unit is assessed simultaneously, can the achievement of each unit be separately tracked?)

- learners with specific needs (do assessors need to adapt assessment methods?)

- number of learners to assessors (allocating learners to assessors should be fair, assessors should not be overloaded)

- problem areas or units (assessors might interpret them differently, or learners might have problems achieving them)

- qualification or criteria to be assessed (are assessors familiar with these; are standards about to be revised?)

- types of records to be completed (manual or electronic).

Activity

Write a strategy for the subject you will internally quality assure. Consider what you will need to do and how you will do it. If you are not currently quality assuring, create a hypothetical strategy. Are there any implications for your job role because of the particular subject you will IQA?

IQA sampling

Once you have your strategy, you will need to use your organisation's proformas to create your plans. The plans will show the activities and sampling that you will carry out over a period of time. If plans are not available you will need to design your own, perhaps based on those in this chapter.

As a minimum, you will need:

- an observation plan

- a meeting and standardisation plan

- a sample plan and tracking sheet.

You could have separate plans for each activity if there are a lot of assessors and learners, or combine them if numbers are small. Your plans should show continual activity over the period of assessment. If IQA is carried out towards or at the end of the assessment process there is little opportunity to rectify any concerns or issues. There are lots of variables to take into consideration when creating your plans. For example, the experience and location of your assessors, the number of learners they have, the complexity of what is being assessed, the use of witnesses, etc. You need to consider all of this in your strategy before planning your IQA activities.

Observation plan

You should observe each assessor over a period of time to ensure they are carrying out their role effectively, supporting their learners adequately, making correct decisions and giving developmental feedback. When planning to observe, you will need to take into consideration their experience, the number of learners they have and the different locations where they assess. When you have built up confidence in an assessor's performance, you could carry out fewer observations. If you have inexperienced or newly qualified assessors you might want to observe them more. If you plan well in advance and liaise with your assessor as to what they will be assessing, you can ensure you cover a variety of units from the qualification or aspects being assessed.

Observing the same unit across different assessors will aid the standardisation process. You might find your assessors do things quite differently and this way you will be able to discuss ways of ensuring consistency of practice. It is the ideal time after an observation to talk to learners and witnesses and you should maintain records of these discussions. A visual planner, as in Table 4.1 below, helps everyone see when the various activities will take place. Specific dates can then be added according to the assessor activities, and an observation report completed. If learners and witnesses are interviewed after the observation, a report should also be completed. Examples of reports can be found in Chapter 5.

Table 4.1 shows a plan for observing four assessors, two of whom have already been observed and the dates added to the plan.

Example

Observation plan – 2012 Level 2 Customer Service					IQA: H Rahl							
Assessor	Jan	Feb	Mar	Apr	May	Jun	Jul	Aug	Sep	Oct	Nov	Dec
P Jones qualified	Unit 101 31.01.12						Unit 102					
M Singh qualified		Unit 101 18.02.12						Unit 103				
J Smith unqualified			Unit 101						Unit 104			
S Hans newly qualified				Unit 101						Unit 105		

Table 4.1: Example observation plan

Meeting and standardisation plan

Regular team meetings between all assessors and IQAs should take place to discuss general issues regarding progress. A plan will reflect when these will take place and ensure staff are available to attend. An agenda should be issued in advance and minutes taken and distributed after the meeting. If someone cannot attend, they should be given a copy of the minutes and be given the opportunity to discuss the content with you at some point. Meetings could take place virtually via teleconferencing if not everyone can attend at the same location. Meetings could also be visually recorded and viewed later by anyone who was absent.

Part of the IQA process is to ensure assessors are standardising their practice. These activities can be timetabled to take place as part of the meeting or as a separate event. Besides the standardisation of assessment practice, if there is more than one IQA for a subject, they should meet to ensure the consistency of their IQA practice, systems and records. IQAs can therefore meet separately from their assessors for their own standardisation activities.

If there is only one assessor, they won't have the opportunity to standardise with other assessors. You could double assess one of their units, enabling a discussion to take place to ensure you are both interpreting it in the same way. If you have double assessed a unit, you cannot then IQA it. Alternatively, your assessor could link up with assessors from other organisations to help standardise their practice, perhaps as part of a consortium.

Example

Meeting and standardisation plan 2012											
Level 2 Customer Service										IQA: H Rahl	
Activity	Jan	Feb	Mar	Apr	May	Jun	Jul	Aug	Sep	Oct	Nov	Dec
Assessor team meeting	4th		9th		7th		6th		8th		10th	
Assessor standardisation activity		16th Unit 101		13th Unit 102		15th Unit 103		17th Unit 104		12th Unit 105		
IQA team meeting			18th			29th			17th			3rd
IQA standardisation activity				22nd				30th				

Table 4.2: Example meeting and standardisation plan

If your qualification is externally quality assured, the awarding organisation will need you to maintain thorough records of meetings and standardisation activities. See Chapter 2 for further details of assessment standardisation and an example pro-forma. A visual planner, as in Table 4.2 on page 142, will help everyone see when the various activities will take place.

Sample plan and tracking sheet

A sample plan and tracking sheet will identify what you will sample, from whom and when. It should also track the dates when interim and summative sampling has taken place. This allows an audit trail to be followed by any EQAs or inspectors. The plan should cover all assessors, what they are assessing and the assessment methods used. You should look at all aspects of the qualification or criteria being assessed on a continuous basis. Some areas you sample might be incomplete and other areas will be complete. This will enable you to see how learners are progressing and monitor how long they are taking to achieve. There is no need to sample something from every learner unless there is a particular reason to do so, for example, a concern about an assessor's decisions.

You will need to sample a cross-section of work from assessors, learners, methods and decisions. To decide on what to sample and from whom, you should consider factors such as:

- assessors – qualifications, experience, workload, caseload, locations
- learners – particular requirements, ethnic origin, age, gender, locations
- methods – observation, questions, witness testimonies, tests, RPL, products, etc.
- decisions – assessment records, VACSR.

Once you are familiar with the above, you can plan your sample using an appropriate method. There are various sampling methods you could use; some are more effective than others. The terminology relates to how they are viewed on the sample plan, such as:

- diagonal (one area from all learners)
- horizontal (something from all areas over time)
- percentage (e.g. 10 per cent from each assessor or learner)
- random (unsystematic method)

- theme based (relating to a particular activity such as work products, witness testimonies, etc.)
- vertical (the same area from each learner).

Example

Sample plan and tracking sheet					
Level 2 Customer Service Assessor: P Jones					IQA: H RAHL
Learner and location	Unit 101	Unit 102	Unit 103	Unit 104	Summative
Ann Bex X Company	Jan *Sampled on 12 Jan 2012*	Feb *Sampled on 18 Feb 2012*	Aug	Sept	Oct
Eve Holler X Company	Jan *Sampled on 12 Jan 2012*	Feb *Sampled on 18 Feb 2012*			
Terri Frame Y Company	July		Mar		
Jon Vanquis Z Company	July			Apr	
Naomi Black Z Company	July				May

Table 4.3: Sample plan and tracking sheet

Table 4.3 shows a mixture of diagonal, horizontal and vertical sampling for four units of a qualification from one assessor and their learners. Two of the units have already been sampled. The IQA will sample all the evidence provided for each unit. The summative sample ensures all documentation is complete.

Whichever methods you choose, they should be fit for purpose and ensure that something from each assessor is sampled over time. You are looking for quality, not quantity. A mixture of diagonal, horizontal and vertical sampling is best as it ensures everything will be reviewed over time. Percentage and random sampling are not good practice as aspects can easily be missed. However, they can be used in addition to other methods, such as theme-based sampling, if a problem is found and you need to sample further. If an assessor covers several locations, work from learners at each location must be sampled to ensure standardisation and fair practice.

Sampling everything from everyone (e.g. 100 per cent sampling) is time consuming and is not good practice. It becomes double assessment rather than quality assurance and doesn't improve or enhance the assessment process.

Once the sample has taken place, a report must be completed and the findings shared with the assessor. An example report can be found in Chapter 5. The actual date of the sample can then be added to the plan to show an audit trail from planning to completion.

It is the IQA's choice what they sample and when, for example, theme-based sampling for witness testimonies from unit 101, assessment plans and feedback records from unit 102, witness testimonies from unit 103, everything from unit 104, etc. The dates for sampling should tie in with the learners' progress. There's no point planning to sample unit 101 in January if no one is working towards it. Regular communication with your assessors will help you keep track of what is taking place and the plan can be updated or amended at any time. Team meetings are also a good opportunity for assessors to give you an update of their learners' progress. It is your choice what to sample, not the assessor's.

Extension Activity

Look at the bullet list of six sampling methods on pages 143 and 144 and state the advantages and limitations of each, in respect of the subject you will be internally quality assuring. Which methods will you use and why?

Maintaining and improving the quality of assessment

If you have a good robust quality system, you will sustain the reputation of your subject or qualification as well as that of the awarding organisation (if applicable). Carrying out observations of your assessors, sampling their learners' work, the assessment decisions and records, will all help ensure IQA is an effective, valid and reliable process.

You must maintain an audit trail of everything you do. If you plan to IQA something in March and don't sample it until April, that's absolutely fine. However, the actual date you carried out the activity must be added to the plan. Having *March* on the sample plan but *12 April* as the actual sampled date is reflecting reality. Not everything will occur when you planned it, perhaps due to holidays, the late submission of work, absence or illness, etc. If you do change any dates, don't be tempted to alter them or use correction fluid. Just cross out one date and write in another so that the original can still be seen. If you save your plans electronically, resave the changes as a different version so that you can access the previous versions if required. You might need to justify to your EQA the reasons why there have been changes.

To help improve the quality of assessment, you need to ensure your assessors are maintaining their occupational competence for the subject area they are assessing. You also need to make sure they are fully competent with your organisation's systems and procedures and assessment practice in general. If your assessors are qualified they will be operating at the required standard to support their learners. If you have assessors that are currently working towards an assessor qualification, their decisions may need to be countersigned by another qualified assessor in the same subject area. As the IQA, you cannot do this as you will then be sampling their assessed work, which is a conflict of interest. However, as the IQA, you will need to ensure all countersigning has correctly taken place when sampling the work of unqualified assessors. Your awarding organisation will be able to give you further guidance on this.

When a new assessor commences at your organisation, you will need to induct them to ensure they understand their job role and the requirements of what will be assessed. The following points are useful to cover with new staff, and with existing staff from time to time:

- tour of the organisation and visit to assessment locations
- introductions to assessors/IQAs and other relevant staff
- organisation's policies and procedures, vision and mission statement
- assessment strategy and assessment documentation
- internal and external quality assurance procedures
- the qualification standards or criteria to be assessed
- details of learners
- curriculum vitae and qualifications checked; CPD record maintained
- sample signature and identification checked
- target date set for achieving the assessor qualification, if applicable

- countersignatory identified if assessor is unqualified

- other aspects such as access to resources, photocopying, administrative support, travel expense claims/pay claims, etc.

You should also discuss the training and development needs of your assessors to ensure they are keeping up to date with their knowledge and practice. This process will identify any requirements they have, which can then be met through CPD. Improving your assessors' performance should lead to an improvement in the quality of assessment.

Example

Philip had been assessing the same qualification for a number of years, but had missed the latest team meeting where the recently revised standards had been discussed. Paula, the IQA, assumed Philip would be fine and had forgotten to send him a copy of the minutes. However, during a chance meeting with Philip she quickly realised he was not aware of a lot of the changes. As a consequence, his learners were not producing the required evidence for one of the units. Paula quickly arranged for Philip to meet with another assessor to update his knowledge and standardise his practice.

Other aspects which might need improving include the records used for the IQA and assessment process. It might be that two forms are currently being used which could be merged into one form, or some questions on a form are no longer relevant. A standardisation activity could be arranged to review and update all the documentation and records used. It's useful to include the date or a version number on each document as a footer, and keep a separate list of the document name, date and version number for tracking purposes. That way, you can quickly see if your assessors are using the most up-to-date version.

Example

Molly sampled the assessment documents used for unit 104 from each of her four assessors. She found one of the assessors had used completely different documentation to the other three. Molly random sampled further units from this assessor and found the same. She was then able to give developmental feedback to the assessor that they were not using the current versions.

Encouraging staff to access documents electronically from a central system when they need them, rather than keeping a stack of hard copies, will help ensure they are using the most-up-to-date version.

The role of ICT in internal quality assurance

Information and communication technology (ICT) can be used to support and enhance the IQA process. This is particularly useful when the IQA is located in a different area from the assessors. A virtual learning environment (VLE) or electronic portfolio could be used to upload learners' work and assessors' records. This would enable the IQA to sample various aspects remotely at a time to suit. Reports could then be completed electronically, uploaded to the VLE or e-mailed to the assessor.

Communication through e-mail or web-based forums can simplify the contact process between the IQA and assessors. There will be times when people are not available at the same time, either for a meeting or a telephone call. Using ICT enables messages to be left which can be responded to when convenient.

Meetings and standardisation activities could also take place remotely, for example, through video conferencing or webinars. Everyone does not need to be in the same room at the same time for activities to be effective. Materials could be produced and circulated electronically prior to the remote meeting and then discussed when everyone is accessible.

Never assume that staff are familiar with how to use the various aspects of ICT. Training sessions may need to be carried out and resources might need to be updated.

Other ICT quality assurance aspects include:

- using a mobile phone/smart phone or digital camera to record an assessor activity. This is useful if the IQA cannot be present at the time – the assessor could make a recording and send it to the IQA

- using web conferencing to talk to learners and witnesses if they are quite a distance from where the IQA is based

- using webinars to view presentations or software packages, enabling participants to remain in their own locations rather than travel to a central location

- recording verbal information, making podcasts or visual recordings of conversations, meetings and/or information regarding updates and changes

- taking digital recordings or videos of role-play activities, or case studies, for example, assessor decisions and developmental feedback. Assessors could view them remotely to comment on strengths and limitations of a particular method

- making visual recordings of how to complete documents and reports. If an assessor is unsure how to fill in a form they could access a video to see an example.

Some of these can be e-mailed to staff or uploaded to an intranet or VLE for staff to access in real time or at a time to suit. See Chapter 3 for the role of ICT in the assessment process.

Activity

Consider how you could use ICT for your IQA role. What resources could you use and how would you use them to effectively support the IQA process?

Appeals and complaints

An appeal is usually about an assessment decision, whereas a complaint is more likely to be about a situation or a person. Learners who appeal or complain should be able to do so without fear of recrimination. Confidentiality should be maintained where possible to ensure an impartial outcome, and the learner should feel protected throughout the full process. If anyone does make an appeal or complaint, this should not affect the way they are treated and the outcome should not jeopardise their current or future achievements.

At some point during the assessment process, a learner may wish to appeal against one of your assessor's decisions. There should be an appeals procedure with which learners and assessors are familiar. Information could also be displayed on noticeboards, in the learner handbook, or be available via your organisation's intranet. Learners will need to know who they can go to, and that their issue will be followed up. This will involve various stages and have deadlines, such as seven days to lodge an appeal, seven days for a response, etc. and all stages should be documented. Usually, an appeals process is made up of four stages: assessor; IQA; manager and EQA (if applicable). As an IQA, it might be your role to monitor appeals from learners and it could be that at the second stage in the appeals process you will need to make a decision whether to uphold the learner's appeal. If you do not uphold it, it will then escalate to the next stage, i.e. your manager. The manager's decision could be final, or if the qualification is externally quality assured, it might then escalate to the EQA, whose decision should be final. The nature of the appeal can be used to inform future practice to prevent further appeals.

Example

Cheng had lodged a formal appeal regarding his assessor's decision for unit 301. He felt he should have passed as he had supplied all the required evidence. Julia, the IQA, spoke to the assessor and reviewed Cheng's evidence. It transpired that the assessor was correct in asking for a further piece of evidence. Julia spoke to Cheng and explained that four pieces of evidence were required and he had only submitted three. He accepted Julia's decision and agreed to supply a further piece of evidence.

If Cheng had used the first stage of the process and discussed it with the assessor first, there would have been no need to involve the IQA. Some organisations will provide a pro-forma for learners to complete, which ensures all the required details are obtained, or encourage an informal discussion with the assessor first. Statistics should be maintained regarding all appeals and complaints; these will help your organisation when reviewing its policies and procedures, and should be provided to relevant external auditors if requested.

Complaints might also be made from one of your assessors against something you have or have not done as an IQA. You could have an assessor appeal against a decision you have made, for example, if you disagreed with one of their judgements. There should be a formal appeals procedure for assessors, similar to the one for learners. However, if possible, try and discuss it with your assessor first to reach an amicable outcome.

Having a climate of respect and honesty can lead to issues being dealt with informally, rather than procedures having to be followed which can be upsetting for both parties concerned.

Extension Activity

Locate, read and summarise your organisation's policies and procedures for appeals and complaints in your particular subject area. Are there any pro-formas supplied and what are the time limits? If your qualification is accredited, find out what role the awarding organisation plays regarding appeals.

Evaluation

Evaluation is not another term for assessment; evaluation is a way of obtaining feedback to improve performance. This can be in the form of surveys or questionnaires (paper based or online), reviews, appraisals and informal and formal discussions and meetings. Feedback can come from learners, assessors, IQAs, EQAs and others such as witnesses and employers. Information gained from evaluations should lead to an improvement for learners, your assessors, yourself and your organisation. Never assume everything is going well just because you think it is or no one has made a complaint.

Information to help you evaluate assessment and IQA practice includes statistics such as enrolment, retention, success and achievement rates. These can affect the amount of funding received or future targets. Feedback from meetings and standardisation activities can also influence the way you evaluate the IQA process. For example, you might decide to redesign some of the assessment documentation or the way that forms are completed, e.g. electronically rather than on paper.

Any patterns, issues or trends and areas of good or poor practice you have identified throughout the IQA process should be summarised and fed back to your assessors.

Evaluation of practice and systems can improve the service everyone receives and contribute to future planning within the organisation.

Surveys and questionnaires

These are useful ways of formally obtaining feedback from everyone involved in the assessment and IQA process. If you use them, you need to consider what you want to find out, who you will ask and why. Don't just ask questions for the sake of issuing a questionnaire and don't just give them to those you know will give a positive response. Everyone should be given the opportunity to be involved and left to decide if they wish to respond or not.

When writing questions, you need to gauge the language and level to suit your respondents. You might be able to use jargon or complex terms with assessors, but not with others. The type of question is also crucial as to the amount of information you require. Using a *closed* question, i.e. a question only requiring a yes or no response, will not give you as much information as an *open* question, which enables the respondent to give a detailed answer.

Example

Did you receive a detailed assessment plan? YES/NO

Was the assessment activity as you expected? YES/NO

Was your assessor supportive? YES/NO

These closed questions would not help you to understand what it was that your learner experienced, and they might just choose 'yes' to be polite. It would, however, be easy to add up the number of yes and no responses to gain *quantitative data*. The questions would be better rephrased as open questions to encourage learners to answer in detail. This would give you *qualitative data*, therefore giving you more information to act on.

Example

How detailed was your assessment plan?

What was the assessment activity and why was it used?

How supportive was your assessor?

Using questions beginning with *who, what, when, where, why* and *how* (WWWWWH) will ensure you gain good quality answers. If you would rather use questions with yes/no responses, you could ask a further question to enable the learner to elaborate on why they answered yes or no.

Example

Was the assessment activity as you expected? YES/NO

Why was this?

This enables the learner to expand on their response, and gives you more information to act on. When designing questionnaires, use the KISS method: *Keep It Short and Simple*. Don't overcomplicate your questions, for example, by asking two questions in one sentence, or make the questionnaire so long that learners will not want to complete it.

You could consider using the Likert (1932) scale, which gives respondents choices to a question such as:

1. Strongly disagree
2. Disagree
3. Neither agree nor disagree
4. Agree
5. Strongly agree

However, you might find respondents choose option 3 as a safe answer. Removing a middle response and giving four options forces a choice:

1. Strongly disagree
2. Disagree
3. Agree
4. Strongly agree

Anonymity should be given for any survey or questionnaire used. If the respondent is with you at the time, this will not be the case; the same goes for telephone or face-to-face questioning. Electronic questionnaires that are e-mailed back will denote who the respondent is, however, postal ones will not. There are lots of online programs for surveys that will guarantee anonymity and will also analyse the results of quantitative data.

Activity

Design a short questionnaire that could be used with learners. Consider the types of questions you will ask and how you will ask them, based upon the information you need to ascertain. Decide how the questionnaire will be implemented, e.g. paper based, online, in person, etc. If possible, ask your assessors to use it with their learners by a set date, analyse the results and recommend improvements to be made based on these.

Searching the internet will give you lots of ideas regarding questionnaire design or programs that could be used to create an online survey.

Always set a date for the return of any surveys and don't be disappointed if you don't get as many replies as you had hoped. Denscombe (2001) predicted a 30 per cent response rate which isn't very high. However, if you give learners time to complete a questionnaire, perhaps immediately after an observation, they will hand it in straight away rather than take it away and forget about it.

Always inform your respondents why you are asking them to complete the questionnaire and what the information will be used for. Make sure you analyse the results, create an action plan and follow this through, otherwise the process is meaningless. Informing the respondents of the results and subsequent action keeps them up to date with developments, and shows that you take their feedback seriously.

Another way of obtaining feedback is through *focus groups* – a face-to-face group meeting and discussion. This could be carried out via teleconferencing if not everyone can attend a certain venue at the same time.

Focus groups show signs of taking over from questionnaires ... they share with postal questionnaires the advantages of being an efficient way of generating substantial amounts of data. However, as with questionnaires, these perceived advantages are offset by considerable disadvantages. For example, it is difficult or impossible to follow up the views of individuals and group dynamics or power hierarchies affecting who speaks and what they say.

(Robson, 2002, p284)

As an IQA you could gain informal feedback from your assessors after an observation. This will help you realise how effective you were and what you could improve in the future. It may also help you identify any problem areas, enabling you to do things differently next time. You could also encourage your assessors to gain informal feedback from their learners after they carry out an assessment activity, for example, during a one-to-one conversation or a group discussion.

Always make sure you do something with the feedback you receive, to help improve the product or service offered to everyone involved in the assessment and IQA process.

Self-evaluation

Self-evaluation is a good way of continually reflecting upon your own practice to ensure you are carrying out your role effectively. When evaluating your own practice, you need to consider how your own behaviour has impacted upon others and what you could do to improve.

A straightforward method of reflection is to have an **e**xperience, then **d**escribe it, **a**nalyse it and **r**evise it (EDAR). This method incorporates the WWWWWH approach and should help you consider ways of changing and/or improving.

Experience → Describe → Analyse → Revise (EDAR)

- Experience – a significant event or incident you would like to change or improve.

- Describe – aspects such as who was involved, what happened, when it happened and where it happened.

- Analyse – consider the experience deeper and ask yourself how it happened and why it happened.

- Revise – think about how you would do it differently if it happened again and then try this out if you have the opportunity.

As a result, you might find your own skills improving, for example giving more effective, constructive and developmental feedback to your assessors.

Reflection should become a habit, for example, mentally running through the EDAR points after a significant event. As you become more experienced and analytical with reflective practice, you will progress from thoughts of *I didn't do that very well,* to aspects of more significance such as *why* you didn't do it very well and *how* you could change something as a result. You may realise you need further training or support in some areas therefore partaking in relevant CPD should help.

There are various theories regarding reflection. Schön (1983) suggests two methods:

- reflection in action

- reflection on action.

Reflection *in action* happens at the time of the incident, is often unconscious and allows immediate changes to take place. It is about being *reactive* to a situation and dealing with it straight away.

Reflection *on action* takes place after the incident and is a more conscious process. This allows you time to think about the incident, consider a different approach, or to talk to others about it before making changes. It is about being *proactive* and considering measures to prevent the situation happening again in the future.

Example

Aalia was observing Pete, an assessor, with a group of learners in a welding workshop. She noticed one of them was not wearing a visor correctly, which could lead to an accident. She immediately went over to the learner and showed him how to wear it the right way. This enabled her to deal with the situation at once. On reflection, she felt she should have asked Pete to deal with the situation with his learner. When giving Pete feedback after the observation, Aalia gave him additional advice on the importance of health and safety.

Part of reflection is about knowing what you need to change. If you are not aware of something that needs changing, you will continue as you are until something serious occurs. Maintaining your CPD, keeping up to date with developments in your subject area, changes in legislation, changes in qualification standards and developments with ICT will assist your knowledge and practice. If you haven't already done so, joining a professional association such as the Institute for Learning (IfL) will give you lots of benefits as well as access to resources and events.

Extension Activity

Reflect upon a recent meeting you have chaired or attended. Evaluate how the meeting went, how you reacted to situations and what you could do differently next time. Consider what CPD you might need to help you with your IQA role.

Summary

In this chapter you have learnt about:

- key concepts and principles of internal quality assurance
- roles and responsibilities of an internal quality assurer
- sample planning and the collection of information
- maintaining and improving the quality of assessment
- evaluation.

Evidence from the completed activities, plus the following, could be used towards the *Principles and practices of internally assuring the quality of assessment* unit, for example:

- written statements cross-referenced to the TAQA unit's assessment criteria

- answers to questions/assignments issued by the awarding organisation

- records of discussions with your assessor.

Cross-referencing grid

This chapter contributes towards the following three TAQA IQA units' assessment criteria. Full details of the learning outcomes and assessment criteria for each TAQA unit can be found in the Appendices.

TAQA unit	Assessment criteria
Principles and practices of internally assuring the quality of assessment	1.1, 1.2, 1.3, 1.4 2.1, 2.2, 2.3 3.1, 3.2 4.1, 4.2, 4.3 5.1 6.1, 6.2, 6.3, 6.4
Internally assuring the quality of assessment	1.1, 1.2 2.3, 2.4 3.2 4.1, 4.2 5.1, 5.3, 5.4
Plan, allocate and monitor work	1.1, 1.2, 1.3, 1.4 3.1

Theory focus

References and further information

Belbin, M (1993) *Team Roles At Work.* Oxford: Elsevier Science and Technology.

Boud, D (1995) *Enhancing Learning Through Self-assessment.* London: Kogan Page.

Denscombe, M (2001) *The Good Research Guide.* Buckingham: Open University Press.

Likert, R (1932) A Technique for the Measurement of Attitudes. *Archives of Psychology* 140: 1–55.

Ofqual (2008) *Regulatory Arrangements for the Qualifications and Credit Framework*. Coventry: QCA.

QCA (2006 Revised) *NVQ Code of Practice*. London: Qualifications and Curriculum Authority.

Robson, C (2002) *Real World Research* (2nd edition). Oxford: Blackwell Publishers.

Sallis, E (2002) *Total Quality Management in Education* (3rd edition). Abingdon: Routledge.

Schön, D (1983) *The Reflective Practitioner*. London: Temple Smith.

Wallace, S (2007) *Achieving QTLS: Teaching, Tutoring and Training in the Lifelong Learning Sector* (3rd edition). Exeter: Learning Matters.

Wood, J and Dickinson, J (2011) *Quality Assurance and Evaluation in the Lifelong Learning Sector*. Exeter: Learning Matters.

Websites

Data Protection Act (2003): http://regulatorylaw.co.uk/Data_Protection_Act_2003.html

Freedom of Information Act (2000): www.legislation.gov.uk/ukpga/2000/36/contents

Health and Safety Executive: www.hse.gov.uk

Institute for Learning: www.ifl.ac.uk

Learning and Skills Improvement Service: www.lsis.org.uk

Qualifications and Credit Framework: http://tinyurl.com/447bgy2

Surveys and questionnaires (free program): www.surveymonkey.com

CHAPTER 5
INTERNALLY ASSURING
THE QUALITY OF
ASSESSMENT

Introduction

In this chapter you will learn about:

- internal quality assurance planning

- monitoring activities and decision making

- providing feedback to assessors

- record keeping – internal quality assurance

- external quality assurance

There are activities and examples which will help you reflect on the above and will assist your knowledge of how to internally assure the quality of assessment. Completing the activities will help you to gather evidence towards the TAQA *Internally assuring the quality of assessment* unit. At the end of each section is an extension activity to stretch and challenge your learning further.

At the end of the chapter is a list of possible evidence which could be used towards the TAQA *Internally assuring the quality of assessment* unit.

A cross-referencing grid shows how the content of this chapter contributes towards the three TAQA units' internal quality assurance criteria. There is also a theory focus with relevant references, further information and websites to which you might like to refer.

Internal quality assurance planning

As soon as you are appointed as an internal quality assurer (IQA) you should find out if there are any other IQAs in the same subject area as yourself. If so, you can communicate with them to find out what you need to do. You should then get in touch with your assessors to introduce yourself to them, for example, at a team meeting. You should have a job description which will help you understand the requirements of your role and you should familiarise yourself with it. If you don't have a job description, then following the requirements of the TAQA IQA units will ensure you are performing your role adequately. You will also need a copy of what will be assessed and internally quality assured, i.e. the qualification standards or job specification, along with copies of the assessment and IQA documentation. Before carrying out any planning and monitoring of assessor practice, you will need to check the following:

- Have all assessors received a copy of the qualification standards or job specification?

- Are there any areas which might cause concern, i.e. aspects which are difficult to achieve or involve complex activities?

- Are all assessors qualified and experienced? You may need to check that their CVs and certificates conform to any requirements.

- Do any assessors need to take an assessor qualification or gain any further experience? If so, you may need to arrange training and development activities for them. You may need to ensure unqualified assessors have their decisions countersigned by a qualified assessor.

- Are there adequate policies and procedures such as appeals and complaints? If not, you may need to produce them and ensure assessors and learners are familiar with them.

- Is there a suitable IQA rationale and strategy? If not, you will need to create one or update the previous one.

- Have learners been allocated to assessors? If not, you need to do this fairly according to each assessor's location and workload.

- Are the assessment and IQA documentation and pro-formas suitable or do they need updating? If there aren't any, you will need to create them. Examples are given here and in Chapter 4.

Once you have all the information and documentation you need, you can begin to plan and monitor assessor practice. You should have the support of the management within your organisation and have sufficient time and resources to perform your role effectively. If not, this could jeopardise the quality assurance process and disadvantage learners.

Monitoring activities and decision making

You should plan to regularly monitor the activities that your assessors carry out, along with the decisions they make. This is to ensure they are performing their job role correctly and not disadvantaging their learners in any way. You will also need to satisfy the requirements of the awarding organisation if you are internally quality assuring an accredited qualification. If you are monitoring the work of assessors who are assessing employees in the workplace, you might also be required to report to their manager.

When planning the activities to carry out, you should base them on the risk factors you have identified in your strategy, for example, the experience of your assessors or any problem units.

Activities that you should plan to carry out include:

- observing assessor practice
- talking to learners
- sampling assessed work and records
- arranging formal meetings
- arranging standardisation activities.

Observing assessor practice

A good way of ensuring your assessors are performing adequately is to see them in action. Not only will this give you the opportunity to see them making assessment decisions, but you will also be able to talk to the learners afterwards. Documenting your observations on a checklist like the one in Table 5.1 opposite will help to ensure you remain objective when making decisions regarding your assessor's competence.

When arranging to carry out an observation, you will need to make sure the learner is aware that you are not observing them, but their assessor. Your assessor, and indeed their learner, might be nervous about being observed. You will need to help them relax and explain you are there to help and support, not to be critical of them. You need to ensure your assessor is performing their job role correctly and making valid and reliable assessment decisions. You also need to check that the area is safe and that any resources used are appropriate.

Talking to learners

After observing your assessor, it's an ideal time to talk to their learner and gain feedback regarding the assessment process. A checklist can be used for this purpose, as in Table 5.2 on page 164. Always give the learner the opportunity to ask you any questions and to discuss any aspects of the assessment and IQA process with you. If you are not able to answer any questions from the learner, make sure you find out and then get back to them. Thank the learner for their time and wish them well with their future progress. Don't be tempted to tell them anything about their assessor's practice, or make excuses for any problems. You can then give feedback to your assessor away from the learner. This should take place as soon as possible after the observation and in an appropriate location. If you or the assessor has any other commitments at the time, a quick verbal account can be given and then a date and time arranged for formal feedback.

It could be that you identify some areas for development, in which case you will need to discuss this sensitively with your assessor and reach an agreement on how to proceed. You should always follow up any action points you set to ensure they have been met and then update the observation checklist accordingly.

Example

Assessor observation checklist				
Assessor: IQA:				
Units/aspects assessed: Location of assessment:				
Checklist	**YES NO N/A**	**Action required**	**Target date**	**Achieved**
Was the learner put at ease and aware of what would be assessed?				
Was an appropriate assessment plan in place?				
Were the resources and environment healthy, safe and suitable for the activities being assessed?				
What assessment activities were used?				
Were questions appropriate and asked in an encouraging manner?				
Were current and previous skills and knowledge used to make a decision?				
Was constructive and developmental feedback given and documented?				
Was the assessor's decision correct?				
Did the learner's evidence meet VACSR requirements? (*valid, authentic, current, sufficient and reliable*)				
Were all assessment records completed correctly?				
Did the assessor perform fairly and satisfactorily?				
Does the assessor have any training needs? If so, how can these be addressed?				
Does the assessor have any questions?				
Feedback to assessor:				
IQA signature: **Date:** **Assessor signature:** **Date:**				

Table 5.1: Assessor observation list

Example

Learner discussion checklist				
Assessor: IQA: Units/aspects assessed: Location of assessment: Learner:				
Checklist	**YES NO N/A**	**Action required**	**Target date**	**Achieved**
Are you aware of your progress and achievements to date?				
Did you discuss and agree an assessment plan in advance?				
Did you have a copy of, and understand what you are being assessed towards?				
Did you have an initial assessment?				
Were you asked questions to test your knowledge and understanding?				
Did you receive helpful feedback?				
Is your progress regularly reviewed?				
If you disagreed with your assessor, would you know what to do?				
Do you have any learning needs or require further support?				
Do you have any questions?				
Feedback to assessor:				
IQA signature: **Date:** **Assessor signature:** **Date:**				

Table 5.2: Learner discussion checklist

Sampling assessed work and records

An excellent way of monitoring assessor practice and decisions is to sample the work they have assessed from their learners. You should have a plan to show what you will sample, from whom and when (see Chapter 4 page 144 for an example). This should be on an interim and summative basis; interim is part way through the learner's progress and summative is at the completion stage. If a problem is identified at the interim stage, there is a chance to put it right. Interim sampling can look at aspects of assessment and learner evidence. Summative sampling can check the full assessment process has been completed successfully and that all documents are signed and dated correctly.

The benefits of interim sampling give opportunities to monitor:

- all assessment types and methods, whether they are safe, valid, fair and reliable or need changing
- consistency between assessors and assessment locations
- good practice that can be shared between assessors
- how assessors are completing their records
- how effective assessment planning is
- how effective feedback to learners is
- how learners are progressing
- if assessors need any support or further training
- if learners need any support or have any particular requirements
- if there are any problems that need addressing before the learner completes
- the views of others, e.g. learners, employers and witnesses
- whether the learner has been registered with the awarding organisation (if applicable, as any assessments prior to registration might be classed as invalid by an awarding organisation)

The benefits of summative sampling give opportunities to check:

- all documents are fully completed and signed by all parties
- all requirements have been met enabling certification to be claimed
- assessors have implemented any action points
- the assessment decisions are correct
- the evidence is valid, authentic, current, sufficient and reliable
- there are adequate assessment plans and feedback records

Making a decision

When sampling work, you are not re-assessing or re-marking it, but making a decision as to whether it meets the assessment requirements. You are ensuring the assessor's plans and feedback records are documenting all the activities, and that their decisions are correct. You might agree with your assessor, in which case you can give them feedback as to what they have done well. You might agree, but feel your assessor could have given more developmental feedback to their learner. You can then give your assessor appropriate feedback as to how they could develop and improve. Alternatively, you might disagree with an assessor's decision and refer the work back to them. If this is the case, you would need to be very explicit as to why the work had not met the requirements and give your assessor advice on how they can support their learner's achievement. Assessors should never do any work for their learners, but help them see how they can achieve it for themselves. You might decide to sample more work from this assessor for the same aspect, to see if it was a one-off, or if the same issue has occurred with other learners. If you find that other assessors are having the same problems with a particular aspect, you can discuss it with all the assessors to help standardise their interpretation of the requirements. Otherwise, the learners might be disadvantaged due to no fault of their own.

Another quality assurance term is internal moderation. If an area of a learner's work is sampled and there are problems, all the learners' work for that area will need to be referred back to the assessor. It could be that it was just an issue with one learner; however, it could be that the assessor had misinterpreted something which resulted in all the learners making the same mistake.

When sampling learners' work, you should always read the accompanying assessment plans and feedback records and any other assessment records such as observation reports and witness testimonies. Reviewing all the assessment documentation will help you gain a clear picture of learner progress and achievement. If witnesses are used, you should contact a sample of them to confirm their authenticity and that they understand what their role entails. If a qualification relies heavily on the use of witness testimonies as evidence, then you will need to carry out adequate training and give support.

While sampling learner work, you can also sample the assessment records. You should check that an assessment plan and appropriate feedback records have been completed correctly. Check they are legible and confirm what has been achieved. You should compare different assessors' records to ensure they are completing them in a standardised way. Some assessors might be very brief with their comments and others quite comprehensive. If this is the case, then the assessor who only writes brief comments might not be fully supporting their learner. You could take copies of some records, remove the assessors' names and use them during a standardisation meeting to agree a consistent approach.

When sampling work you must complete a report of what you have reviewed. Make sure you keep a note on your sample report of anything you have asked your assessor to do, so that you can follow it up by the target date. Always update your records to reflect what was sampled and when, and when any action has been met. A clear audit trail of all IQA activities must be maintained to assist compliance and transparency. It also helps in the event of an appeal or complaint.

Table 5.3 overleaf is an example of an internal quality assurance sample report.

When sampling work from different assessors, if you are sampling the same units from a qualification, programme or aspects of a job specification, you can see how consistent the different assessors are. You can then note any inconsistencies to discuss at the next team meeting. For example, if one assessor is giving more support to learners, or expecting them to produce far more than others, then this is clearly unfair.

Sampling learners' work is also a good opportunity to check for aspects such as plagiarism and copying. It could be that two learners have submitted a piece of work which is almost identical. You would need to satisfy yourself that they hadn't worked together or copied one another's work. You and your assessors need to be aware of learners colluding or plagiarising work, particularly now that so much information is available via the internet. Learners should take responsibility for referencing any sources for all work submitted, and may be required to sign an authenticity statement to confirm the work is theirs. If you suspect plagiarism, you could type a few of their words into an internet search engine or specialist program and see what appears. You would then have to refer it to your assessor to challenge their learner as to whether it was accidental or otherwise.

Activity

Find out what your organisation's policy is regarding cheating, copying and plagiarism, and find out what your involvement would be as an IQA. Ensure all your assessors are aware of the policy and discuss any issues at your next team meeting.

Example

Internal quality assurance sample report		
Learner: Qualification:		
Assessor: IQA:		
Interim/summative (*please circle*)		
Unit/aspects sampled	**Comments**	**Types of evid‹ sampled**
Is the evidence:	If no – action required and target dates:	Date completed
Valid? YES/NO		
Authentic? YES/NO		
Current? YES/NO		
Sufficient? YES/NO		
Reliable? YES/NO		
Have assessment plans and records been completed, signed and dated?		YES/NO
Is the assessor's decision correct?		YES/NO
Summative IQA – can the certificate now be claimed?		YES/NO
Feedback to assessor:	Assessor's response:	
IQA signature: Date: Countersignature: Date: (*if required*)		

Table 5.3: Internal quality assurance sample report

When sampling, you need to make sure all work is valid, authentic, current, sufficient and reliable (see Chapter 4 for details). If you are in any doubt, you must refer it back to your assessor, or have an informal discussion with them. It might be that the assessor has omitted to state something on their feedback record or it might be more serious. Never feel pressured to agree with your assessor if you feel something is not quite right. If there are other IQAs in the same subject area as yourself, you could discuss your findings with them first.

You will also be making decisions as to whether the assessment types and methods used are adequate, fair and appropriate. If one assessor is carrying out three observations with all their learners, but another is only carrying out one, then that is clearly not fair. If one assessor is expecting some learners to write a 2,000-word essay, and others a 1,500-word essay, then again, that's not fair. Your assessor might justify their actions by saying they are challenging the more able learners, however, unless the assessment requirements state this is acceptable, then it isn't.

Because you are only sampling aspects of the assessment process, there will be some areas that get missed. This is a risk as you can't sample everything from everyone. You need to build up your confidence in your assessors to know they are performing as they should. If you find a problem when sampling, or have any concerns, you will need to increase your sample size. Conversely, you could reduce the sample size for your experienced assessors if you have confidence in them. However, never assume everything is fine as experienced assessors could become complacent. If all your assessors know what you will be sampling and when, they might not be as thorough with the areas you are not due to sample. You can always carry out an additional random sample at any time and ask to see an aspect of assessor practice which isn't on your original plans.

After a period of sampling, you should analyse your findings and give overall feedback to your assessors, perhaps at the next team meeting. You might have found patterns or trends, for example, all assessors are making the same mistake with a particular unit. You might see that one assessor is taking more time than others to pass their learners, or that several of their learners have left. Conversely, you might find another assessor whose learners are completing really quickly and you will need to find out why.

Arranging formal meetings

You should have a plan to reflect when you will hold meetings with your team of assessors. If you can plan the dates a year in advance this will ensure everyone knows when they will take place and therefore be able to attend. If you have a large team you could hold a meeting every month or a smaller team less often. You could use an agenda, like the one in Table 5.4 below, to ensure all important aspects of the assessment and IQA process are covered.

Example

AGENDA

IQA and assessor team meeting

(Qualification)

(Date)

1. Present
2. Apologies for absence
3. Minutes of last meeting
4. Matters arising
5. Programme: recruitment, new starters, changes to standards
6. Assessment: record keeping, methods used, current progress of learners, issues or concerns, CPD activities
7. Internal quality assurance – observations and sampling dates, registrations and certifications, appeals and complaints, general IQA feedback
8. External quality assurance – feedback and reports
9. Standardisation – feedback from recent activity
10. Equality and diversity
11. Health and safety
12. Any other business
13. Date and time of next meeting

Table 5.4: Example agenda

The agenda could be circulated in advance by e-mail or be uploaded to your organisation's intranet. It might be your responsibility to chair the meeting and take minutes. If so, try and type them up as soon as possible after the meeting. Always ensure everyone who attends, or was absent, receives a copy or can access them electronically.

Communication

People act differently depending upon the situation they are in and the people they are with at the time. You might find that on a one-to-one basis an assessor is quite mature but in a meeting can be rather disruptive and immature.

Berne's (1961) Transactional Analysis Theory is a method of analysing communications between people. Berne identified three personality states; the *child*, the *parent* and the *adult*. These states are called *ego states* and people behave and exist in a mixture of these states, due to their past experiences, gestures, vocal tones, expressions, attitudes, vocabulary and the situation at the time.

Transactional Analysis assumes all past events, feelings and experiences are stored within, and can be re-experienced in current situations. You might see this with assessors who take on a different state depending who they are with. For example, acting like a child and asking for help from a particular colleague, but acting like an adult with a different colleague.

Transactions are verbal exchanges between two people: one speaks and the other responds. If the conversation is complementary then the transactions enable the conversation to continue. If the transactions are crossed, the conversation may change its nature or come to an end.

Berne recognised that people need *stroking*. Strokes are acts of recognition which one person gives to another. This can be verbal words of appreciation, and strokes can be positive or negative. Giving or receiving positive strokes develops emotionally healthy people who are confident in themselves and have a feeling of being *okay*.

Example

Ibrahim was working towards his IQA qualification and wanted to prove how good he was, as well as please his assessor. He kept saying to himself, I'll be okay if I gather all the required evidence to please my assessor and don't make mistakes. By doing this, Ibrahim felt he would be looked upon more favourably and receive strokes of approval in the form of positive feedback, which would encourage and motivate him.

Understanding a little about the different states of the child, parent and adult will help you see how your assessors take on different roles in different situations, particularly in meetings where some may be more vocal than others.

If you ever feel like a *child* at work, it may be because your manager is operating in their *parent* mode and you are responding in your *child* mode. Your *child* makes you feel small, afraid, undervalued, demotivated and rebellious. These feelings may make you undermine, withdraw, gossip, procrastinate, plot revenge or attempt to please in order to be rewarded. In this *child* mode, you cannot become a successful professional.

As you are in a managerial role, you may find yourself acting like a *parent*. You may have learnt this from your parents' responses to you years ago. The *parent* mode makes you feel superior, detached and impatient. Being in this state can make you harden your tone, not listen to people, shout, bribe others into complying, and criticise them more than you encourage them.

The best option is to be in the *adult* state. As an *adult*, you feel good about yourself, respectful of the talents and lives of others, delighted with challenges, proud of accomplishments and expectant of success. These feelings make you respond to others by appreciating and listening to them, using respectful language, perceiving the facts, considering alternatives and having a long-term view and enjoyment of work and life.

If you realise that you have moved into a *role*, it is possible to change if you need to.

When you feel your *child mode* about to make you withdraw, gossip or undermine, you can choose instead to participate, find out the facts and resolve your differences in the *adult* state.

When you feel your *parent mode* about to make you criticise, threaten, bribe or take over, you can choose instead to speak warmly, be patient, listen and find enjoyment in the challenge.

It is very difficult to consistently be in the *adult* state. You may find yourself adapting to different situations and responding to the states other people have taken on. However, trying to remain in the adult state should help you gain confidence and respect from your assessors.

Arranging standardisation activities

You will need to plan and manage standardisation activities with your assessors and any other IQAs. You could have separate events for assessors and for IQAs (if there is more than one IQA for your subject). Standardisation of practice ensures the assessment and IQA requirements are interpreted accurately, and that everyone is making comparable, fair and consistent decisions.

Aspects which can be standardised include:

- assessment activities – looking at safety and fairness, validity and reliability, deciding alternative methods for particular learner requirements or needs

- creating a bank of assessment materials, i.e. assignments, multiple choice questions, etc.

- how assessors interpret the assessment requirements and standards and how they make their decisions

- how learner evidence meets the requirements

- the way assessment plans and feedback records are completed

- the way feedback is given to learners

- the way learner reviews are carried out

- the way witness testimonies are used

- updating assessment and IQA documentation, i.e. checklists, records and pro-formas.

One way to standardise practice between assessors is to ask them each to bring along a unit or aspect they have assessed with the supporting assessment records. These can be swapped between assessors who can then re-assess them. The activity could be anonymous if learner and assessor names are removed beforehand. A discussion can then take place to see if all assessors are interpreting the assessment requirements in the same way and making the same decisions. This is also a chance to see how different assessors complete the forms, and the amount of detail they write. The activity can lead to an action plan for further training and development of assessor practice.

Assessment types and methods should also be standardised. If one assessor has written a project or assignment for their learners to carry out, they should share it with other assessors. This will ensure all learners have access to the same assessment materials. It's also a chance to make sure the questions are pitched at the right level for the learners.

Example

Shane had produced an assignment for his learners which would holistically assess two units from a level 1 numeracy qualification. Part of the assignment expected learners to reflect upon their progress. When the assignment was discussed by the assessor team at a standardisation meeting, it was felt that the learners might not be skilled enough to reflect adequately. It was also noticed that an aspect of one of the units had been missed in the assignment. The team decided that reflection would not be used formally. Shane rewrote the assignment and e-mailed it to his colleagues for further feedback before use.

All assessment activities used must be fit for purpose. Formative assessments are often informal and not usually counted towards the achievement of a qualification. They can therefore be more flexible to cater for different learner needs and their progress at the time, for example, using a quiz with learners to check knowledge gained at a given point. Summative assessments are formal and are either produced by the awarding organisation or by the assessor, for example, a test. If more than one assessor is involved for the same subject, they should get together to standardise all activities and materials created and used.

Records will need to be kept of all standardisation activities and show that all units or aspects have been covered over a period of time.

See Table 2.4 in Chapter 2 for an example of a standardisation record for assessed work.

Extension Activity

Create plans for observing your assessors, holding meetings and standardisation activities, and for sampling learner work (examples are in Chapter 4). If you have the opportunity, carry out some activities and analyse how effective your IQA plans and documents were and what changes you would make and why.

Providing feedback to assessors

You should provide verbal feedback to your assessors whenever you get the opportunity. Formal feedback could be given after an observation of their practice, after sampling their assessed work, or during an appraisal or meeting. This should always be followed up with written feedback. Informal feedback can be given at any time to help confirm your assessors' practice and development. It can enable your assessors to see what they are doing right, and what they can do to improve. Formal feedback should be given at an appropriate date, time and place, and in a constructive and develop-mental manner. Always remember that it is unprofessional to give feedback to an assessor in front of their learners. You should also give your assessor a copy of any report you have completed. This acts as a formal record of feedback and any action required, which you should follow up.

Feedback should be regarding the assessment process and not be critical of the assessor as a person. It should be used to confirm competence, and to motivate and encourage rather than apportion blame for any reason. Above all, it should be to help your assessor develop their assessment practice, and to maintain and improve the quality of assessment for their learners.

If you find something that the assessor has done wrong, or that they could improve upon, don't be critical but state the facts. You could ask your assessor to reflect upon their performance before you give feedback. That way, they might realise their mistakes before you have to point them out. You can then suggest ways of working together to put things right. It could be that your assessor was unaware of something they should or should not have done. Communicating regularly with them and identifying any training needs should prevent problems from occurring.

You might not find anything wrong, in which case you still need to give feedback, which will be positive and confirm that what they are doing is right. If you have an assessor who is performing really well, you could ask them to mentor an underperforming or new assessor, if they have time.

Always allow your assessor time to clarify anything you have said and to ask questions. Don't interrupt them when they are speaking and avoid jumping to any conclusions. Use eye contact and listen carefully to what they are saying. Show that you are a good listener by nodding your head and repeating key points. Your assessor should leave you knowing exactly what needs to be done and by when.

Example

Sarah sampled six assignments that John had marked from his group of 30 learners. She found his handwritten records difficult to read and his feedback to his learners very sparse. However, all the learners had met the criteria and produced some really good work. When Sarah gave feedback to John, she began with something positive and then moved on to the developmental points: John, I enjoyed reading your learners' assignments and I felt they had all put in a lot of effort. However, I do feel that your feedback to them is not as detailed as it could be, and I found your writing hard to read. Could you word-process your feedback, and take the opportunity to state something specific regarding each learner's achievement?

This example shows how John could improve his feedback skills to help his learners. It was also given in an encouraging manner. The use of the word *however* to link the points is much better than the word *but*, which can sound negative.

Feedback should always be:

- based on facts and not opinions, and aimed at assessors not learners
- clear, genuine and unambiguous
- developmental – giving examples for improvement or what could be changed
- documented – records must be maintained
- focused on the activity not the person
- helpful and supportive – guiding the assessor to useful resources and CPD activities
- honest, specific and detailed regarding what was or wasn't carried out
- positive and constructive – focusing on what was good and how assessment practice can be improved or changed
- specific and detailed regarding what was sampled and what was found
- strategic – seeking to improve the assessor's performance.

Please see Chapter 2 for information on different feedback methods such as evaluative or descriptive, constructive or destructive, and objective or subjective.

Activity

Carry out various IQA activities such as observing assessors. Consider what went well, what problems you encountered and what you would do differently to improve the process for yourself and your assessors.

Neuro Linguistic Programming

Neuro Linguistic Programming (NLP) is a model of interpersonal communication concerned with relationships and experiences. It can be useful when providing feedback to assessors to help influence their development. NLP is a way to increase self-awareness and to change patterns of mental and emotional behaviour. Richard Bandler and John Grinder, the co-founders of NLP in the 1970s, claimed it would be instrumental in finding ways to help people have better, fuller and richer lives. They created the title to reflect a connection between neurological processes (neuro), language (linguistic) and behavioural patterns (programming) which have been learned through experience and can be used to achieve specific goals. The model was based on how some very effective communicators were habitually using language to influence other people.

NLP training should help turn negative thoughts into positive thoughts. It provides the skills to define and achieve outcomes, along with a heightened awareness of the five senses.

> *NLP is an attitude which is an insatiable curiosity about human beings with a methodology that leaves behind it a trail of techniques.*
> Richard Bandler (co-creator of NLP;
> www.inlpf.com/whatisnlp.htm, accessed 15.08.11)

> *The strategies, tools and techniques of NLP represent an opportunity unlike any other for the exploration of human functioning, or more precisely, that rare and valuable subset of human functioning known as genius.*
> John Grinder (co-creator of NLP;
> www.inlpf.com/whatisnlp.htm, accessed 15.08.11)

NLP techniques can be used to:

- coach assessors how to gain greater satisfaction from their contributions
- enhance the skills of assessors

- improve own and others' performance

- improve an individual's effectiveness, productivity and thereby profitability

- set clear goals and define realistic strategies

- understand and reduce stress and conflict.

NLP provides questions and patterns to make communication more clearly understood, for example, all thoughts and behaviours have a structure, and all structures can be re-programmed. Do you use jargon, complex terms or clichés without thinking? Your assessors might not understand what you are talking about because you assume they already have the knowledge. To improve your feedback skills, you could observe others who are skilled and experienced to see how they perform.

Activity

Arrange to observe an experienced IQA, preferably in your subject area, to watch how they interact with their assessors. Are they using any NLP techniques to make communication easier? If you can't carry out an observation, watch or listen to influential people on the television or radio. Ask yourself what it is about them that makes them successful. Can you emulate this in yourself? If so, how?

Emotional intelligence

Emotional intelligence (EI) is a behavioural model, given prominence in Daniel Goleman's book *Emotional Intelligence* (1995); however, work originally began on the model in the 1970s and 1980s by Howard Gardiner.

Goleman identified five domains of emotional intelligence:

- knowing your emotions

- managing your emotions

- motivating yourself

- recognising and understanding other people's emotions

- managing relationships, i.e. the emotions of others.

The principles of EI provide a new way to understand and assess people's behaviour, attitudes, interpersonal skills, management styles and potential. This could be useful if you have a large team of assessors who aren't always working in a consistent manner. By developing emotional intelligence Goleman suggested that people can become more productive and successful at what they do, and help others to be more productive and successful too. He also suggested that the process and outcomes of developing emotional intelligence contain aspects which are known to reduce stress for individuals and organisations. This can help improve relationships, decrease conflict, and increase stability, continuity and harmony.

Emotional intelligence has been described as:

> The ability to perceive emotions, to access and generate emotions so as to assist thought, to understand emotions and emotional knowledge, and to reflectively regulate emotions so as to promote emotional and intellectual growth.
>
> (Salovey and Sluyter, 1997, p197)

Becoming aware of your own emotions and how they can affect your activities will help you develop more fulfilling and professional relationships with your assessors.

The EI concept argues that IQ (Intelligence Quotient), or conventional intelligence, is too narrow as there are wider areas of emotional intelligence that dictate and enable how successful people are. Possessing a high IQ rating does not mean that success automatically follows.

Demonstrating and evaluating your interpersonal and intrapersonal skills should help you deal effectively with situations which might occur with your assessors.

Extension Activity

Carry out an observation of one of your assessors giving feedback to one of their learners. Was it given in a supportive and encouraging way? Was it specific and did it confirm the learner's competence and leave them with developmental points? After the learner has gone, give feedback to your assessor in a developmental way. Afterwards, evaluate how you gave the feedback and whether you would have done it differently, based on NLP and EI models. You could ask for comments from your assessor to help you.

Record keeping – internal quality assurance

It is important to keep records to satisfy company, quality assurance, awarding organisation and regulatory authorities' audit requirements. This will usually be for a set period, for example three years, and should be the original records, not photocopies or carbon copies, to guarantee authenticity. Records should always be accurate, dated and legible. To create a visual audit trail of everything you review you could use a coloured pen to date and initial all assessment records and learner work that you sample. The dates on these records should agree with the dates on your tracking sheets, checklists and reports.

Types of IQA records you might maintain include:	Other records you might maintain include:
• assessor observation checklists • internal quality assurance sample reports (interim and summative) • IQA rationale and strategy for your subject area • learner discussion checklists • minutes of meetings • observation plan, meeting and standardisation plan, sample plan and tracking sheet • questionnaire or survey results with evaluations and actions • standardisation activities. • witness discussion records	• details of assessors and IQAs, e.g. their CVs, CPD records and copies of certificates • enrolment, retention, success and achievement statistics • equal opportunities data • external quality assurance reports, inspection reports and actions taken • records of appeals and complaints • records of learner registration and certification details with an awarding organisation (if applicable) • self-assessment reports.

Table 5.5: IQA records

There may be a standardised approach to completing the records, for example, the amount of detail which must be written, or whether the records should be completed manually or electronically. You will need to find out what your organisation expects you to do.

You must ensure your assessors are keeping the required records for their learners (see Chapter 2 for details). All records should be kept secure and should only be accessible by relevant staff. You also need to ensure you comply with organisational and statutory guidelines such as the Data Protection Act (2003) and the Freedom of Information Act (2000).

Extension Activity

Create a file (either manual or electronic) for all the records you will need to maintain as an IQA. Make sure the plans you use have version numbers and that all completed documents are dated. Compare the records you need to maintain with those in Table 5.5 opposite. Is there anything else you need to keep? What organisational or regulatory requirements must you follow regarding record keeping and why?

External quality assurance

If your qualification is externally quality assured a member of the relevant awarding organisation will visit to ensure you are compliant with their requirements, assessment and quality assurance strategies. They will be known as an external quality assurer (EQA) or external quality consultant. If there are not many learners and your EQA has confidence in your systems, they might carry out a remote sample rather than visit. This means you will post learners' work, assessment and IQA records to them, or give them remote access to electronic portfolios and records.

Never be concerned about making contact with your EQA. They are there to help ensure the qualification is assessed and internally quality assured in accordance with their requirements. They would not want you to do anything that contravenes any regulations. You should share all advice and support you receive with your assessors and managers.

Your EQA should give you plenty of notice of their visit or remote sample. You will need to ensure everything they request is available. You should also have an extra sample of learners' work available in case they ask to see it.

Prior to their visit, you will need to liaise with your assessors to obtain all the required information and data, and to make sure previous action plans have been met. The EQA may want to observe you give feedback to your assessors, or see an assessor in action with a learner. They will also want to see all the assessment and IQA records.

During the visit, the EQA will usually:

- check that claims for certification are authentic, valid and supported by auditable records
- complete a report, identify and agree any relevant action

- confirm that assessments and IQA activities are taking place and are conducted by appropriately qualified staff (they may need to see CVs, certificates and CPD records)

- check that any previous action has been met

- ensure compliance with the approval and qualification criteria

- ensure procedures are followed, including access to fair assessment and appeals

- ensure that national standards are being consistently maintained

- follow an audit trail through all assessment and IQA records

- give advice and support regarding the interpretation of standards

- give advice regarding appropriate CPD opportunities

- observe and sample assessment and IQA practice

- read minutes of meetings and check standardisation records

- recommend actions for non-compliance if requirements are not met

- report any malpractice to the awarding organisation

- talk to learners and others involved in the assessment process

What the EQA carries out will depend upon how much activity is taking place and how much of a risk there is with the qualification. EQA reports will usually state whether your organisation is low, medium or high risk for your particular subject area. If your organisation is operating at a low risk, you will have direct claims status, which means you can request certificates for successful learners when they complete. However, you will need to keep all your records in the meantime for the next EQA monitoring activity. If you have a medium or high risk rating you will receive an action plan and may not be able to claim certificates or register new learners until the actions have been met.

After you receive the report, you should hold a meeting with your assessors to discuss any issues and action points. Some action points might relate to your own training and development needs. Make sure you are keeping up to date with developments in your subject area, and in IQA practice in general. Other action points might relate directly to the qualification delivery, assessment and quality assurance. It might be your responsibility to ensure the action is carried out, or you might delegate aspects to others. Always keep track of progress and update your EQA.

Between visits, you can contact your EQA for advice and support. Don't leave any issues until their next visit, as problems could occur which might be too late to correct. You should always inform your EQA when there are any changes in areas such as staff or systems.

There are other external bodies that will advise and monitor quality assurance; these will depend upon which area of the UK you are working in and whether your organisation receives external funding.

They include:

- funding agencies
- local authorities
- Office for Standards in Education, Children's Services and Skills (Ofsted)
- Office of Qualifications and Examinations Regulation (Ofqual).

By remaining proactive and dealing with issues before an official visit, you should alleviate any major concerns during a visit.

Extension Activity

Obtain the name and contact details of the EQA who has been allocated for your qualification (if applicable). Obtain and read their last report, see what your risk rating is, and find out when they are next due to visit. Check what action points or comments they made and ensure that you are following them.

If you are not quality assuring a qualification, ask your manager for their most recent report regarding assessment and IQA practice in your organisation. Is there anything you need to do or improve? If so, make sure you do it and communicate any changes to your assessors.

Summary

In this chapter you have learnt about:

- internal quality assurance planning
- monitoring activities and decision making
- providing feedback to assessors
- record keeping – internal quality assurance
- external quality assurance.

Evidence from the completed activities, plus the following, could be used towards the *Internally assuring the quality of assessment* unit, for example:

- IQA rationale and strategy for your subject area
- observation plan, meeting and standardisation plan, sample plan and tracking sheet
- two completed assessor observation checklists
- two completed learner discussion checklists
- four completed internal quality assurance sample reports
- minutes of two meetings
- records of two standardisation activities
- reports from EQAs and actions taken (if applicable)
- CPD record
- written statements cross-referenced to the TAQA units' assessment criteria
- answers to questions issued by the awarding organisation
- records of discussions with your assessor.

Cross-referencing grid

This chapter contributes towards the following three TAQA IQA units' assessment criteria. Full details of the learning outcomes and assessment criteria for each TAQA unit can be found in the Appendices.

TAQA unit	Assessment criteria
Principles and practices of internally assuring the quality of assessment	1.1, 1.2, 1.3, 1.4 2.1, 2.2, 2.3 3.1, 3.2 4.1, 4.2, 4.3 5.1 6.1, 6.2, 6.3, 6.4
Internally assuring the quality of assessment	1.1, 1.2 2.1, 2.2, 2.3, 2.4, 2.5, 2.6 3.1, 3.2 4.1, 4.2 5.1, 5.2, 5.3, 5.4
Plan, allocate and monitor work	1.1, 1.2, 1.3, 1.4 3.1, 3.2 4.1, 4.2

Theory focus

References and further information

Berne, E (2010) *Games People Play: The Psychology of Human Relationships*. London: Penguin.

Goleman, D (1995) *Emotional Intelligence*. London: Bloomsbury.

Salovey, P and Sluyter, D (1997) *Emotional Development and Emotional Intelligence: Educational Implications*. New York: Basic Books.

Wood, J and Dickinson, J (2011) *Quality Assurance and Evaluation in the Lifelong Learning Sector*. Exeter: Learning Matters.

Websites

Association for Neuro Linguistic Programming: www.anlp.org

Data Protection Act (2003): http://regulatorylaw.co.uk/Data_Protection_Act_2003.html

Emotional Intelligence: www.unh.edu/emotional_intelligence/index.html

Freedom of Information Act (2000): www.legislation.gov.uk/ukpga/2000/36/contents

Ofqual: www.ofqual.gov.uk

Ofsted: www.ofsted.gov.uk

Plagiarism: www.plagiarism.org and www.plagiarismadvice.org

CHAPTER 6
PLAN, ALLOCATE AND
MONITOR WORK

Introduction

In this chapter you will learn about:

- producing and using a work plan

- identifying and allocating responsibilities to team members

- monitoring the progress of others and the quality of their work

- communication skills

- updating the work plan

There are activities and examples which will help you reflect on the above and will assist your understanding of how to plan, allocate and monitor work. Completing the activities will help you to gather evidence towards the TAQA *Plan, allocate and monitor work* unit. At the end of each section is an extension activity to stretch and challenge your learning further.

This chapter relates to the management of others and as such contains various leadership, management and communication theories.

At the end of the chapter is a list of possible evidence which could be used towards the TAQA *Plan, allocate and monitor work* unit.

A cross-referencing grid shows how the content of this chapter contributes towards the three TAQA units' internal quality assurance criteria. There is also a theory focus with relevant references, further information and websites to which you might like to refer.

Producing and using a work plan

If you lead a team of internal quality assurers (IQAs) and/or assessors you should be in a managerial role and as such have the authority to go with it. You will need to plan, monitor and review their progress and the quality of their work within that context. Producing and using a work plan will help you organise the various activities you need to carry out to ensure they take place. A work plan is a visual reminder of what needs to be done and by when. You might create a work plan for yourself, and one for various team members if you are delegating activities to them. Monitoring and reviewing the activities will ensure appropriate progress is made towards agreed targets. The activities should lead to an improvement in quality and standards for the product or service being offered. Records should always be maintained and kept for audit purposes, for example, by managers, external quality assurers (EQAs), and inspectors such as Ofsted or funding agencies.

Your aim should be that your own work, and the work of your team, is carried out effectively. Your starting point will be your job description or role specification. This should state what you are expected to do, enabling you to create a work plan and put it into action. If you don't have a job description or role specification, working towards the TAQA IQA units will ensure you are performing your role adequately.

Activity

Have a look at the TAQA standards in Appendix 6 on page 228. Look at the learning outcomes and assessment criteria to see what you need to do to perform this role.

Information you need to help you create a work plan includes:

- details of your team members, what their experience, knowledge and skills are and what they are expected to do and by when

- documentation, policies and procedures being used

- external organisation requirements if you are working with accredited qualifications

- financial information such as budgets for carrying out various IQA activities, or funding requirements

- information regarding the qualification/job specification or areas being assessed and internally quality assured

- job specification – for yourself and others you are responsible for

- organisation vision and mission

- priorities, targets and expected success criteria

- resources: physical and human, environmental and transport

- the locations of your team members, assessors and learners.

Using the *who, what, when, where, why and how* (WWWWWH) approach will help you create your plans. All activities you set should have objectives which are SMART, i.e. specific, measurable, achievable, realistic, and time bound.

Example

Activity – to observe the practice of all IQAs.

Objective – to observe each IQA twice a year by using an agreed checklist.

The objective is therefore specific by stating the task to be carried out (an observation) and measurable (by using a checklist). It will be achievable by the observer, is realistic and relevant to their job role and is time bound as it will be carried out twice a year.

If you carry out internal quality assurance activities as well as manage a team of IQAs you will already be using some types of work plan such as:

- an observation plan

- a meeting and standardisation plan

- a sample plan and tracking sheet.

These plans are good for the various aspects of the IQA process and you can see examples in Chapter 4. However, you might have other responsibilities which need to be planned for, or activities you need to delegate to others. An overall work plan will help you prioritise and keep track. All activities and objectives should be agreed with your team members and they should have a copy of the plan in manual or electronic format. The work plan in Table 6.1 opposite is a basic example for an IQA. The shaded area denotes the month the activity should be carried out, the actual date of the activity can then be added when known.

Example

Objective	To plan, monitor and review the IQA process in accordance with organisational requirements												
IQA name:	H Rahl												
Activities 2012	Jan	Feb	Mar	Apr	May	Jun	Jul	Aug	Sep	Oct	Nov	Dec	Comments
Write annual IQA report for directors	25th												
Attend annual management meeting	31st												
Review all assessment and IQA documentation		15th											
Prepare for EQA visit			18th										
Meet with EQA				1st									Reserve a room
Review assessment/IQA policies/ procedures													
Carry out staff appraisals													
Produce IQA observation plan													
Plan meeting dates for assessors and IQAs													
Plan standardisation activities													
Create IQA sampling plan													
Produce report and statistics of appeals/complaints													Could be done in January

Table 6.1: Example work plan

The work plan can be produced and updated electronically, or it can be printed and displayed as a visual reminder. If it is electronic, it's best to save any updates as a different version number to allow the original to remain accessible. Alternative styles of work plan could be used such as wall planners which can be purchased from stationers, or templates such as Gantt charts which are available free via an internet search or as part of some computer programs.

As a manager you should be familiar with and committed to the vision and mission of your organisation. You should also know what part you have to play in achieving them. You need to make sure your team members are also aware of how their role fits into the overall organisational requirements, and what they need to do. The vision and mission must be achievable and all staff should understand what they are and be committed to them. However, if they are unrealistic, then staff might not be motivated to achieve them. If the latter is the case, you will need to discuss issues and concerns with someone in authority; otherwise staff morale may become low. This could lead to staff not performing their roles correctly and disadvantaging learners.

Activity

Obtain and read your organisation's vision and mission statements. Analyse how they will impact upon your role in producing a work plan for your area of responsibility. If you don't have a job description, make a list of what you consider your management roles and responsibilities to be. Locate all the relevant policies and procedures that underpin your job role and find out if there is any legislation that you need to follow (e.g. health and safety, equality and diversity, employment law, etc.).

Supporting your team

You will need to know who all your team members are and keep their contact details handy. You might have staff who are employed full time, part time, or on a voluntary or peripatetic basis (i.e. working for several organisations). There will be occasions when you might not all be able to get together at the same time, therefore using electronic methods of communication can ensure you all stay in touch.

You will need an in-depth knowledge of all relevant policies, procedures and documentation that will be used by yourself and your team. You should support your team members in a proactive rather than reactive way, encouraging them to talk to you when they need to. If they have a concern, it will need to be dealt with straight away rather than it escalating into a major problem due to a lack of communication. You might need to carry out coaching and/or mentoring activities with your team members, carry out staff appraisals and training needs analyses, and countersign unqualified IQAs' decisions. These are all managerial roles and you could consider taking a management qualification as part of your continuing professional development (CPD). You might also be responsible for producing and/or updating staff and learner handbooks.

Table 6.2 below lists the skills required to help you perform your job role. If there are any you are uncertain of, you could research them further.

Skills to perform your role and support your team include:	
• analysing	• monitoring
• budgeting	• motivating
• coaching	• planning
• communicating	• prioritising
• consulting	• problem solving
• computing	• providing feedback
• data analysing	• questioning
• decision making	• reading and writing
• delegating	• record keeping
• information and data management	• reviewing
• leadership	• setting SMART objectives
• listening	• speaking
• managing conflict	• stress management
• managing people	• supporting others
• mentoring	• time management

Table 6.2: Job role skills

When planning activities for your team members to carry out, you will need to match their skills, qualities and locations against certain activities, objectives and priorities. You will need to know your staff well to be able to do this, or talk to them to find out their strengths. You might need to work within specific time or financial constraints such as deadlines or lack of a budget. All activities will still need to take place and be monitored but they could be carried out at a different time or location. Your work plan can be updated and amended at any time to take into account any changes or unforeseen events.

The Leitch Review was established in December 2004 to consider the skills profile the UK should aim to achieve by 2020 in order to maximise growth, productivity and social justice. The UK must aim to improve its prosperity and fairness in a rapidly changing global economy. The Review has found that these changes are decisively increasing the importance of skills. Skills are an increasingly central driver of productivity, employment and fairness. The UK must achieve a world class skills base if it is to improve its prosperity and fairness in the new global economy. (Leitch, 2006, p27)

Improving your own skills, and those of your team members will help everyone perform their job roles to the best of their ability and contribute towards CPD. There might be instances where your team members have become demotivated or demoralised by circumstances beyond their control, for example, a recent spate of redundancies. Your own personal qualities and skills can help motivate and enthuse your team members.

Activity

Make a list of the personal skills and qualities you feel you possess. While doing this, consider your roles and responsibilities and the management duties you will be performing. Analyse these and consider how you can develop them further, to achieve the requirements of your job role. You might like to identify your strengths, weaknesses, opportunities and threats – known as a SWOT analysis – and then plan relevant CPD activities. You could also ask your staff members to complete a SWOT analysis to ascertain their strengths.

Some people are naturally good managers, have a helpful and pleasant personality and are good at communicating with others. However, if you have to identify and improve the performance of others and monitor their progress, appropriate training will help. You might also have to deal with staff complaints, appeals and grievances. If this is the case, you must remain objective and maintain confidentiality throughout the process.

Personality styles

Understanding a little about your personality style will help you develop your personal qualities and skills. In the 1950s, a test was devised by cardiologists Friedman and Rosenham to identify patterns of behaviour considered to be a risk factor for coronary heart disease. This placed people as *Type A* or *Type B* and is still used today to analyse personalities. Type A individuals can be described as impatient, excessively time-conscious, insecure about their status, highly competitive, hostile and aggressive, and incapable of relaxation. They are often high achieving workaholics who multitask, drive themselves with deadlines and are unhappy about the smallest of delays. Due to these characteristics, Type A individuals are often described as *stress junkies*. Type B individuals, in contrast, are described as patient, relaxed, and easy-going. There is also a Type AB mixed profile for people who cannot be clearly categorised. Knowing which type you are could help you change if necessary, for example, becoming less stressed.

There are other personality styles tests such as Myers Briggs Type Indicator (MBTI) and Kiersey which are based on the work of Carl Jung (1875–1961). Both involve a self assessed personality questionnaire. An MBTI report will give your preferences for each of four pairs, known as E & I, S & N, T & F, J & P.

1. **E**xtrovert – sociable, get lonely when not surrounded by others, life and soul of the party, need to be the centre of attention, get energy from being with others.

1. **I**ntrovert – territorial, need mental and physical space, pursue activities on their own, can feel lonely in a crowd, often work well with people.

2. **S**ensing – need things to be realistic, trust their experience and senses, down to earth, good at picking out details; often good doctors, nurses, policemen.

2. **I**ntuitive – see things as wholes rather than details, trust hunches, enjoy ideas, challenges and change; good inventors, innovators and pioneers.

3. **T**hinking – make decisions based on principle, logic or objectivity; they like words such as analysis, principle, objective and firmness.

3. **F**eeling – base decisions on their personal impact; they like words such as values, personal, persuasion, appreciation.

4. **J**udging – like things settled, orderly, planned and completed; they make lists and follow them, they get things moving, use systems and routines.

4. **P**erceiving – do not like planning, preparing or cleaning up, are flexible and adaptable, delay making decisions hoping something better will turn up, are spontaneous, open-minded and tolerant

The benefits of the preferences enable you to have some knowledge of how people function, and enable you to realise that other people have aims and needs, feelings and values etc which may differ from your own. Never assume that your team members are as highly motivated or as capable as yourself. Personality style tests should always be confidential and adhere to a code of ethics.

Kiersey's model has four main temperament groups:

- Artisan – concrete in communicating about goals and flexible and accommodating about achieving them.

- Guardian – concrete in communicating about goals, logical, good at facilitating projects.

- Idealist – abstract in communicating, co-operative, good interpersonal skills.

- Rationalist – abstract in reasoning, utilitarian in achieving goals.

The temperament groups can be further subdivided into character types. There are also eight technical terms which are the same as Myers Briggs, for example, extrovert and introvert. The questions used in the test will reveal a person's temperament and character type.

You might like to carry out a personality style test and encourage your team members to do so too. Reviewing your personality type should help you see aspects you might need to change, improve or develop, and can help you become more effective as a manager. Knowing people are of different types should help you realise how individuals act and react in different situations.

Taking personal responsibility for your own actions, supporting your team members and not apportioning blame should lead to a healthy working atmosphere for all concerned. This in turn should lead to an improved service for the learners, and an improved reputation for the organisation.

Extension Activity

Create a work plan for your area of responsibility, along with other plans such as an IQA assessor observation plan. Consider if you will need additional work plans for tasks you will delegate to team members. Decide on the activities that will be carried out along with appropriate objectives and target dates.

Identifying and allocating responsibilities to team members

Once you know who your team members are, along with their experience, knowledge and skills, you can begin allocating responsibilities for various activities. You will, of course, need to identify what the activities are, along with appropriate objectives to enable you to know when they have been achieved. They should be based on the job roles of yourself, your team members and the requirements of the organisation and qualification. If you are leading a team of IQAs you will need to decide what you will do yourself and what you will delegate. It could be that you plan a yearly calendar of assessor meetings and prepare the agendas, but not chair them all. Delegating some meetings to your other IQAs on a rota basis will give them responsibility for the meetings and help them take ownership of agreed actions.

You will need to identify and make a list of all the activities you expect your team members to carry out. You can then discuss SMART objectives to be achieved and create a work plan in conjunction with each person. Wherever possible, you should delegate tasks to your team members based upon their strengths. You could ask your team members to carry out a SWOT analysis to assist this process.

Example

Raj has a team of six IQAs who each have four assessors for the Health and Social Care qualification. One IQA, Cameron, is new and working towards his IQA qualification. Raj could have allocated any of the other three experienced IQAs to countersign Cameron's decisions. However, he allocated Tom due to the fact he was a very patient and approachable person and was also a qualified mentor. Raj felt these strengths would further support Cameron's development and help him achieve his IQA qualification quicker.

You might experience some hostility between your team members, for example, if they feel they should or should not be carrying out various activities. Getting people to work as a team can be problematic, particularly if there is a high staff turnover in your organisation. If this is the case, you would need to find out why staff are leaving and meet with relevant managers in your organisation to do something about it. Gaining feedback from the staff who have left should help you ascertain the reasons.

Group and team working

A group is a collection of individuals and each person will have different ideas and ways of performing. Team building activities can be good fun and lead to staff having a better working relationship with each other. However, some staff may feel they are a waste of time, or there might not be a budget available for them. If you expect your team members to work together collaboratively on certain activities or projects you might like to familiarise yourself with Tuckman's *group formation* theory of forming, storming, norming, performing and adjourning, which he formulated in 1965 and amended in 1975.

Forming – this is the *getting to know you* and *what shall we do* stage. Individuals may be anxious and need to know the boundaries and code of conduct within which the team will work.

Storming – this is the *it can't be done* stage. It's where conflict can arise, rebellion against the leader can happen and disagreements may take place.

Norming – this is the *it can be done* stage. This is where group cohesion takes place and norms are established. Mutual support is offered, views are exchanged and the group co-operates to perform the task.

Performing – this is the *we are doing it* stage. Individuals feel safe enough to express opinions and there is energy and enthusiasm towards completing the task.

Adjourning – this is the *we will do it again* stage. The task is complete and the group separates. Members often leave the group with the desire to meet again or keep in touch.

Being aware of the stages that groups go through, and informing your team members of each, should help you all see why things happen the way they do. Depending upon the activity, the stages might happen over a short or longer term time frame. You might even see all the stages occur during one meeting where the team is new and have a tight deadline for an activity. Or you might have a team that gets stuck at one of the stages and you will need to intervene to move them on.

Activity

Plan an activity that you could use with your team, for example, standardising the initial assessment documentation. Carry out the activity and watch how the team develops through the stages. How many stages did it go through and was the activity achieved within the time allocated? Did you have any staff members who were disruptive, or worked well with particular team members? If so, what could you do next time to ensure everyone is performing on task?

Figure 6.1: Team working needs

Coverdale (1977) stated the essence of team working is that individuals have their own preferred ways of achieving a task, but that in a team, they need to decide on one way of achieving this. In a team, three overlapping and interacting circles of needs have to be focused upon at all times. The *task needs,* the *team needs* and the *individual needs*.

When setting activities for your team members to carry out in groups, consider the following.

To achieve the task ensure:

- a SMART objective or target is stated
- responsibilities are defined
- working conditions are suitable
- supervision is available

To build and maintain the team ensure:

- the size of the team is suitable for the task
- health and safety factors are considered
- consultation takes place
- discipline and order are maintained

To develop the individual ensure:

- responsibilities are defined
- grievances are dealt with

- praise is given

- individuals feel safe and secure

Individual personalities, and the roles that they take on when part of a group, may impede the success or the achievement of the task. As a manager, make sure you supervise your team members' work carefully to keep all individuals focused.

You might need to agree ground rules with your team members when working on group activities. For example, switching off mobile devices and respecting others' opinions to help the group work effectively. If new members join the team, they should be made to feel welcome and introduced to everyone else. Allocating a mentor to them, or acting as a mentor yourself, will help them settle in. Hopefully, they will not feel isolated as they have a named person they can go to with any questions.

As the manager of the team, you should lead by example and promote an environment based on respect. If a team member has made a mistake, don't directly blame them, but find out what went wrong and why. It could be that the same mistake might be made by others. You could use the situation as a learning experience and share your solutions with your team members to ensure it doesn't happen with them too. Your staff should feel comfortable in talking to you about any concerns they have.

Once you get to know your team members and their strengths, you will feel confident at delegating various activities to them. However, never assume they will always be carried out. You will need to monitor what your staff are doing, perhaps by asking them to give you a written, electronic or verbal report at agreed times.

The age range of your team members might affect the way that they work, or their attitudes towards work. The demographics of the country are continually changing. The *veteran* generation (aged 65 plus) may have been with the same employer for a long time and be thinking of retiring, have probably paid off their mortgage, have children who have left home and therefore have different priorities from the other generations.

The *baby boomers* (aged 48–64) might be working fewer hours and increasing their leisure pursuits, have grown-up children and a low mortgage. This generation will increase over the next few years and lead to a larger number of older than younger people in the work place.

Generation X (aged 30–47) might be mid-career, have had several jobs, and perhaps experienced redundancy and unemployment along the way. They might have a large mortgage and a growing family.

Generation Y (aged 18–29) will be first or second jobbers, may still be living with their parents, have few responsibilities and may have a large debt. They use technology a great deal and the line between work and social use can become blurred.

With these different generations come different aspirations, expectations, attitudes and values towards work. You might have team members from the different generations who have experienced these differences first hand. As a result, their attitude might be different towards their peers or indeed towards yourself as their manager.

Example

Marla is an assessor in her late 50s and extremely competent at assessing her subject of Hospitality and Catering. Her organisation wants all staff to use electronic assessment records but Marla is apprehensive as she has not used a computer before. Jon, her IQA, asks another assessor, Robbie, who is in his 20s to help her. Robbie is pleased to do this as he has been using computers for many years. Marla was initially concerned and had even considered leaving, however, she finds she gets on very well with Robbie and also learns how to use an e-mail program and the internet. In return she shares a lot of Hospitality and Catering knowledge with him.

Tamm Communications (www.tcicanada.com), a top 100 Canadian employer, state there are ten different workplace differences between Generations X and Y:

1. Preferred style of leadership
   - **X** – only competent leaders will do.
   - **Y** – collaboration with management is expected.

2. Value of experience
   - **X** – don't tell me where you have been, show me what you know.
   - **Y** – experience is irrelevant, as the world is changing so fast.

3. Autonomy

- **X** – give them direction, and then leave them to it.
- **Y** – questions, questions, questions.

4. Feedback

- **X** – expect regular feedback.
- **Y** – need constant and immediate feedback.

5. Rewards

- **X** – freedom is the ultimate reward.
- **Y** – money talks.

6. Training

- **X** – want to continually learn, if they don't they will leave.
- **Y** – still in an exam driven mentality.

7. Work hours

- **X** – do their work and go home.
- **Y** – will work as long as needed ... or until they get bored.

8. Work life balance

- **X** – they want to enjoy life to the full, while they are young enough to do so.
- **Y** – their lives are busy – they need a lot of *me* time.

9. Loyalty

- **X** – they are as committed as everyone else working there.
- **Y** – already working out their exit strategy.

10. Meaning of money

- **X** – it gives freedom and independence.
- **Y** – just something that allows them to maintain their lifestyle.

One of the greatest differences between Generations X and Y seems to be what they want from work. Generation X is enticed by freedom and independence and get on with their jobs without asking too many questions. Generation Y is more money and lifestyle oriented, focused on their own interests and used to 24-hour access to products and services. Another difference between the two generations relates to the use of technology. Generation Y have been brought up with technology and see it as embedded in, and integral to, their life. They have had the opportunity to use the internet, e-mail and various computer programs at school and expect to use them at home and work. They embrace new technology with ease, expect instant access to information, use social network sites, and often don't have independent thought or retain information as it is so easy and quick to locate it elsewhere. Self-development or self-gain is often part of their motivation and many are reward oriented. To them, their social life comes first. Generation X, in contrast, mainly use technology for convenience, for example, online banking and shopping, but it does not play a big part in their social lives.

A new generation is now growing up known as *Generation Z* (or the *i-generation*, meaning the internet generation). They have had lifelong access to technology, the internet and communication tools such as instant messaging, blogs, text messages, Twitter, online videos and social networking. Access to multimedia to such an extent can lead to a change in communication methods, which to other generations can look like a lack of social manners. Communication becomes via technology rather than face to face and can lead to poor spelling and grammar. Personal aspects often take priority over work due to the *immediate* and *switched on* lives they lead. The opposite may also occur such as the desire to check work e-mails in their own time. This generation has been subjected to a fame culture through the many reality television shows and is often influenced by celebrities and fashion. However, an economic downturn may lead to a change in this generation's attitudes, for example, their concern for the environment; not being as indulgent as their parents were, and recycling and reusing products.

Having an awareness of these differences might help you understand your team members' strengths and limitations. For example, graduates might be academically qualified but be lacking relevant experience. Older people, although very experienced, might not have the technological skills required. Being aware of this will help you appreciate the different aspirations, expectations, attitudes and values of the different age ranges within your team.

Research various management theories regarding team work, for example, John Adair (2002: John Adair's 100 Greatest Ideas for Effective leadership and Management), Meredith Belbin (2010: Team Roles At Work) and Handy and Constable (1988: The Making of Managers). You could compare their similarities and differences. Knowing more of the theories of why individuals act the way they do will help you plan the workload to the strengths of your team members.

Monitoring the progress of others and the quality of their work

You must regularly monitor the progress of your team members to ensure they are performing satisfactorily. Your staff should be aware of what you are monitoring and when. This will be done formally by following your IQA plans for observations, meetings, standardisation activities, and sampling their decisions. Giving them a copy of the documentation you will be using enables them to see what they are being monitored towards. You can also monitor informally by talking to team members and others involved in the assessment and IQA process when you have the opportunity.

When monitoring progress, you will be looking at the quality of work, for example, the amount and type of feedback given by other IQAs to assessors. Records of all formal activities should always be maintained, which can then be used as a basis for improvement and standardisation.

Monitoring progress and giving regular feedback can:

- boost motivation
- build trust and respect
- confirm staff are doing their job correctly
- confirm understanding of the organisation's vision and mission
- help overcome resistance to change
- help to avoid potential problems
- help to build a sense of ownership and responsibility
- identify any training and development needs

- improve communication

- reduce potential conflict

There will be internal and external policies, procedures and legislation which will need to be followed. For example, your organisation might require you to observe every assessor four times per year whether they are experienced or not. You might consider this too much, or you might consider it good practice in that everyone is being treated fairly. You also need to know the limits of your own role and what you can and cannot do in the timeframes.

Besides observations, meetings, standardisation activities and sampling assessed work, there are other monitoring activities you could perform. For example, interviews with learners, employers and witnesses, visits to assessment locations, and staff appraisals.

Whatever monitoring methods you are using, you are ultimately ensuring your staff are being consistent and accurate with their decisions, and interpreting the standards correctly. The learner is the customer and needs to be treated fairly and ethically by everyone who is in contact with them. You also need to make sure everyone understands and complies with all internal and external requirements. This is particularly important if you are quality assuring accredited qualifications from an awarding organisation.

If you have recently had an EQA visit, you will need to discuss the report with your team, along with any action points. You might need to delegate some actions to others or revise the systems and procedures you are using. You could also meet with other staff in your organisation to review the EQA reports for all the different subjects. There might be some patterns identified which would necessitate a change in a policy or procedure.

Although you are managing a team, you also need to ensure your own performance is meeting the required standards. If there are other IQAs in the same subject area as yourself, you can monitor each other. If not, you could ask for feedback from your assessors to help you improve. For example, it could be that you are performing your role adequately, but some assessors feel you need to be more accessible when they have urgent questions. Feedback from your peers and team members can be as valuable as traditional hierarchical feedback.

Activity

How do you seek the views of your team members? Do you have any evidence of seeking their views and acting upon them? You could consider issuing a questionnaire to gain feedback from your assessors regarding the IQA process. The results might help you revise the ways you monitor your team.

When standards are not maintained

Standards might not be maintained due to a lack of knowledge or skills by team members. Identifying any issues early on can enable staff training and development to take place. The issues can then be used to standardise practice within the team. When allocating work, you need to identify any individual skill shortages. This could mean you can't deploy someone as you would like to, or they could be placed in a difficult situation that they can't manage.

Monitoring your team members' performance and progress will help ensure the learners are receiving a good quality service from your organisation. It should also identify any concerns that can be dealt with immediately to alleviate any learner appeals or complaints.

It is good practice to consult your team members regarding the ways you will monitor their performance and agree the expected standards. You also need to be clear about what will happen if they don't meet the standards or are performing poorly. It could simply be a need for further training and development, or it could be a more serious matter.

Unsatisfactory performance

Unsatisfactory performance might be a result of a lack of knowledge or skills on behalf of the individual. This could be their fault, for example, not being honest with regard to their knowledge or skills when they applied for the position. Or it could be the fault of the organisation by not conveying crucial information, for example, when a policy has changed. Recruiting and retaining staff who have the necessary experience, knowledge and skills will hopefully keep staff turnover low. Investing in training and ongoing support for your team members should enable them to carry out their job role effectively. However, there may be times when an individual does not perform satisfactorily.

There should be a policy within your organisation for dealing with unsatisfactory performance, which might lead to disciplinary action if an individual does not conform. If an individual's performance is not up to standard, an informal discussion could take place first to establish the reasons and then agree necessary action. If the action cannot be reasonably achieved due to individual circumstances, the staff member should be given the opportunity of support such as further training or assistance. In more serious circumstances, they could be offered a reduction in their workload, counselling or stress management.

Disciplinary action could occur if the individual's performance constitutes misconduct. A verbal warning could be given and an action plan put in place. If the action is not completed by an agreed date, a written warning could be given. Three written warnings could lead to dismissal in serious circumstances. Throughout all these stages, support should be offered to the individual to help them improve. They should be very clear about what is expected and what will happen if the actions are not met. The process can be linked to performance appraisals and reviews. Formal records should be maintained and relevant employment law followed.

Hopefully, your staff member will improve, make progress and meet the standards. However, if you don't wish to follow your organisation's disciplinary procedure, you might be able to offer them a different job role or look at reducing their workload or hours. There are many reasons why someone might not be performing well and these should all be taken into consideration. You will need to liaise with relevant personnel in your organisation, such as Human Resources, to ensure any contracts and/or terms of employment/equality legislation have not been breached.

Unsatisfactory performance of an individual could reflect badly on you and your organisation. It is therefore important to identify any issues quickly, discover the causes and put an action plan in place to rectify the problem.

Activity

What do you consider to be poor performance and how would you deal with it? What relevant policies are in place for you to ensure the satisfactory performance of your staff?

Armstrong (2003) suggests the following guidelines for defining effective individual performance.

- Measures should relate to results, not efforts.

- The results must be within the individual's or team's control.

- Measures should be objective and observable.

- Data must be openly available for measurement.

- Existing measures should be used or adopted wherever possible

Performance measures should always be discussed during staff appraisals and you should monitor the progress of individuals and teams towards them. There's no point making these measures unobtainable as you could be setting your staff up to fail. You are there to support your staff, not make things difficult for them.

Extension Activity

How do you decide upon the standards of performance for the individuals and teams you have responsibility for? Do you discuss them with your staff and give them a copy? What methods do you use to monitor them and how effective do you think your methods are?

Communication skills

Communication is the key to effective management of your team. The four skills of language are *speaking, listening, reading* and *writing*. Using these effectively in various ways should help with the achievement of the activities you expect your team members to carry out.

Methods of communication include written and oral, for example:

- e-mail, e.g. to quickly pass on information to the full team

- face to face, e.g. meetings or staff appraisals

- intranet, e.g. updated documents, policies and procedures

- newsletters, e.g. bulletins and updates (hard copy or electronic)

- notice boards, e.g. displaying work plans and information for staff

- telephone, e.g. a call to check on a team member's progress

- written, e.g. letters, memos, reports and minutes (hard copy or electronic)

Different methods can be used depending upon the situation or person.

Example

Imran needs to notify his team quickly of a change to a meeting date. He e-mails and sends a text to all the team members. He also telephones two members who he knows do not have direct access to e-mail or text messages. This way he has used several communication methods to meet the needs of his team.

You will need to develop the skills which enable you to use all the methods of communication which are practical, and to decide which is most suitable for a particular situation. You should weigh up the advantages and limitations of the different methods and consider if you need any training, for example, to use new technology. In some cases, more than one method may be needed. For example, you might have an informal discussion with team members and follow this up with an e-mail to confirm what was decided.

The way you communicate with your team might be influenced by your personality. For example, you might prefer to use e-mails rather than the telephone or text messages. Whichever method you use, you need to make sure that what you convey is understood and acted upon. You need to be seen as a respected and trusted source of accurate information. You might not be liked by everyone in your team, however, you are performing a professional role and you are not there to be everyone's friend. Don't take it personally if you feel someone doesn't like you; it's probably the situation they don't like rather than you as a person.

You need to be aware of your verbal and non-verbal body language, for example, not folding your arms when speaking as this could look defensive. You also need to take into account the way you speak and act, as your mannerisms might be misinterpreted by others.

Records should always be maintained of all formal communications. This will enable them to be referred to at a later date, for example, if there is any doubt about what was actually said in a meeting, or if actions which should have been completed have not been. Informal communications can be more personal and may be quicker if you need to get your team members to react immediately to new information. However, not having a record could prove disadvantageous if a team member has no recollection of you asking them to do something. This would be of particular importance if any issues result in disciplinary action.

Skills of communicating effectively include the way you speak, listen and express yourself, for example, with non-verbal language, and the way you construct your sentences. Understanding a little about your own personal communication style will help you create a lasting impression upon your team members.

Interpersonal and intrapersonal skills

A way of differentiating between interpersonal and intrapersonal skills is to regard interpersonal skills as *between people* and intrapersonal skills as *being within a person*. Understanding and using these skills will help you develop a range of creative communication techniques appropriate to the activities you require your team members to perform.

Interpersonal skills are about the ability to recognise distinctions between other people, to know their faces and voices; to react appropriately to their needs, to understand their motives, feelings and moods and to appreciate such perspectives with sensitivity and empathy. Possessing inter-personal skills will help you develop personal and professional relationships.

Ways to improve interpersonal skills include:

- being a mentor to others
- getting organised
- meeting new people at work, social groups, clubs, meetings, etc.
- participating in workshops or seminars in interpersonal and communication skills
- spending time each day practising active listening skills with friends, family, colleagues, etc.
- starting a support/network group

Intrapersonal skills are about having the ability to be reflective and access your inner feelings. Having this ability will enable you to recognise and change your own behaviour, build upon your strengths and improve your limitations. This should result in quick developments and achievements as people have a strong ability to learn from past events and from others.

Ways to improve intrapersonal skills include:

- attending courses, e.g. Neuro Linguistic Programming (NLP), Transactional Analysis (TA), Emotional Intelligence (EI)
- creating a personal development plan
- developing an interest or hobby
- keeping a reflective learning journal
- meditation, or quiet time alone to think and reflect
- observing people who are great leaders, motivators or positive thinkers
- reading self-help books
- setting short- and long-term goals and following these through

Howard Gardner (1993) defines intrapersonal intelligence as: *sensitivity to our own feelings, our own wants and fears, our own personal histories, an awareness of our own strengths and weaknesses, plans and goals.* (Gardner, 1993, p263). He is best known for his theory of multiple intelligences of which there are eight, interpersonal and intrapersonal being two of them. The other six are:

- linguistic – the ability to use language to codify and remember information; to communicate, explain and convince
- logical – also known as mathematical intelligence; the capacity to perceive sequence, pattern and order, and to use these observations to explain, extrapolate and predict
- musical – the capacity to distinguish the whole realm of sound and, in particular, to discern, appreciate and apply the various aspects of music (pitch, rhythm, timbre and mood), both separately and holistically
- naturalist – the ability to recognise, appreciate, and understand the natural world; it involves such capacities as species discernment and discrimination, the ability to recognise and classify various flora and fauna, and knowledge of and communion with the natural world
- physical – also called kinaesthetic intelligence; the ability to use one's body in highly differentiated and skilled ways, for both goal-oriented and expressive purposes; the capacity to exercise fine and gross motor control
- visual-spatial – the ability to accurately perceive the visual world and to re-create, manipulate and modify aspects of one's perceptions

According to Gardner, individuals possess all of these intelligences. However, they are not all present in equal proportions (in extreme circumstances it may appear that an individual is severely lacking in one or more). The particular combination of intelligences and their relative strengths can form a profile that is unique to each individual. Some people are more intelligent than their peers; others appear superior at certain tasks, are more capable of manipulating information or more readily see the solutions to problems. Others are more expressive or more capable of learning new tasks quickly.

Being aware of differing intelligences within your team members, and in yourself, will help you consider alternative ways of communicating with your staff. Gardner's eight intelligences have been debated and amended by many other theorists over time. They can be compared to various learning styles theories, for example, Honey and Mumford's (1986) Activist, Pragmatist, Reflector and Theorist.

Extension Activity

Consider how you will communicate with your team members. Do you prefer a formal or informal approach and why? Review the theories mentioned so far in this chapter and state how they might influence the way you act and react with your staff.

Updating the work plan

Your original work plan will need updating at some point. All changes will need to be communicated to your team members via the next team meeting or by another quicker appropriate method such as telephone or e-mail.

As a manager you should keep up to date regarding what is happening in your area of responsibility and within your organisation. This also means keeping up to date with changes regarding the qualification or aspects being assessed and internally quality assured. If your team are working with accredited qualifications, you will need to ensure they all read the latest updates from the awarding organisation. It's useful to sign up for newsletters and check the website regularly. Any developments should be discussed at team meetings and minutes maintained.

Examples that will necessitate a change to your work plan include:

- an EQA or external report requiring immediate action

- an increase in learners

- changes to funding

- developments with resources, i.e. new technology

- financial or budget constraints

- organisational developments, i.e. additional locations for assessment

- policy and procedural changes

- qualification changes

- staff turnover

- targets not being met

- updated documentation

If you are involved in communications from those in higher positions than yourself, you should be kept up to date with what is happening in your organisation. If you don't attend all the meetings or read e-mails and updates you might not know about any important developments. When changes do occur, it is best that you convey them to your team members rather than have them hear rumours that might not be true, for example, a takeover bid or possible redundancies.

When amending your work plan, try not to use correction fluid, but cross out and rewrite any changes to allow the original information to still be seen. This is useful in case of any queries as to why activities were changed or what the original dates were. If you are using an electronic work plan you can resave it as a different version with a new date. However, do keep a note of which is the latest version in case you accidentally refer to an outdated one.

Your work plans should be regularly reviewed to make sure that they are still fit for purpose, and updated to meet changes and new circumstances. When amending your plans, you are likely to be more successful if you include your team members in the making of major decisions rather than imposing changes upon them. As their job roles will be affected directly, discussing these and communicating with your team on an ongoing basis could help alleviate future problems.

Example

Celina needed to amend her observation work plan for her ten assessors due to her relocation to the company's European site for a month. She sent an e-mail to all those whom she was due to observe during that time giving them a new date for the following month. Almost immediately, she received e-mails from nearly all her assessors stating the dates were not suitable. On reflection, Celina should have asked her team members first for suitable alternative dates. She would then not have had to deal with several annoyed individuals as well as wasting her time making rearrangements.

Communication is a two-way process and at some point you will have to reallocate responsibilities. However, if you can do this by agreement rather than imposition you should maintain the respect and support of your team members. If there are times when you do have to impose a change on an individual, try to do so with tact and diplomacy. Tell your team members why you are making the changes and that you need their support. Some people might resist change as they are comfortable with the way they currently do things. During meetings you could stress that change is inevitable in training and education and that you all need to react to it in a positive way. Treating change as an opportunity for improvement can be enlightening and motivating. Ensuring your team members and yourself remain current in practice should help towards a smoother transition when any changes do take place.

When assessors decide to leave your organisation, you will need to plan who will take over their workload and ensure there is a smooth transition so as not to disadvantage any learners. If the learners are taking an accredited qualification, you will need to inform the awarding organisation of any staff changes.

Feedback and conflict

You should give ongoing informal feedback to your team members as well as formal feedback. If there is a culture of giving constant feedback, your team members are more likely to listen and respond to your comments. Feedback should always be constructive and developmental and should be given individually when possible, and to teams perhaps during a meeting. There is a chance that in some organisations feedback is only given in formal situations such as staff appraisals, after an observation or a sampling activity. If this is the case, individuals might come to dread the formal meeting as they may feel they have done something wrong. Giving praise, and clarifying situations when you have the opportunity will help motivate your staff. Individuals need to know what they are doing right, as well as what they are doing wrong. Creating a culture of giving and receiving regular feedback will help break down barriers, increase motivation and encourage staff to feel valued. This can contribute to positive working relationships and can make more formal feedback sessions, such as staff appraisals, run smoother.

Example

Keiran was walking past a classroom and noticed a group of learners who were becoming rather disruptive. He saw Alfons, the assessor, immediately deal with the situation. When Keiran next saw Alfons in the corridor, he said how pleased he was that the situation had been dealt with in a quick and amicable manner. This left Alfons feeling that what he had done was worthwhile and had been noticed.

According to Kermally (2002) feedback, apart from being ongoing, should also be a development tool. It should allow skills gaps in teams and individuals to be identified, and provide opportunities for the necessary skills to be obtained. Carrying out staff appraisals should be seen as a positive way of discussing a person's job role, any concerns they might have and identifying any training needs. If action points are agreed, these should always be followed up by both parties.

Conflict can arise when an individual or a group believe that someone has done (or is about to do) something with which they disagree. It could be something minor such as an individual sitting in another's usual seat at a meeting. Or it could be more serious, such as a dispute over who carries out certain tasks. There could be challenges and barriers that your staff might face which you weren't aware of, for example, transport issues. This might involve you reallocating staff to make the location more accessible to them. A team member might have a complaint or grievance against another team member and it might be your responsibility to deal with it. You should always base your judgement upon facts after listening to both sides, and be fair and ethical with your decision. Make sure you keep records for reference.

Mullins (2004) identified a range of potential sources of conflict with individuals, groups and organisations.

Individuals may come into conflict because they have different attitudes, personality styles or particular needs. In some instances, the situation might be aggravated by stress or illness. One team member, for example, may perceive quality assurance activities in a different way to another. A reason for different attitudes can be due to the age gaps between different individuals. An older person might feel they have the necessary skills, knowledge and experience, but the power and responsibility might lie with a younger person.

Groups might come into conflict because individuals have different skills, attitudes and ways of working. Team members might interpret tasks in different ways, new staff might feel excluded or a key person might be absent. Organisation characteristics can create conflict, for example, the hierarchy structure, management or leadership styles. This could result in differences and disagreements between departments or teams within the organisation.

Sometimes, simple situations can easily lead to conflict if they are not dealt with immediately or are misinterpreted. Ongoing communication and feedback should help confirm your expectations of your team members, and their expectations of you. Always establish the root cause of any situation that leads to conflict to work out a strategy which will hopefully resolve it. Opportunities should be taken to clarify any misunderstandings and the whole team should be informed to ensure everyone is working to the same ethos. Allowing conflict to worsen over time can lead to a situation becoming much more difficult to resolve. Conflict can also affect others who are not directly involved in the original situation. For example, if you don't take any action, then your own manager might perceive you as being ineffective. This could affect the confidence they have in you as a manager, and it could also affect the respect you have from your team members.

Extension Activity

Refer to your original work plans created earlier on in this chapter. What changes would you make to them now that you have been using them for a while? What developments might occur in the future which would require you to amend them? Will you act differently with your team members now that you have gained knowledge of communication techniques?

Summary

In this chapter you have learnt about:

- producing and using a work plan
- identifying and allocating responsibilities to team members
- monitoring the progress of others and the quality of their work
- communication skills
- updating the work plan.

Evidence from the completed activities, plus the following, could be used towards the *Plan, allocate and monitor work* unit, for example:

- detailed work plans with reviews and amendments
- EQA reports with an analysis of the findings and actions taken
- list of priorities and SMART objectives/success criteria for team members
- list of your own and team members' responsibilities
- records of monitoring and evaluating team members' work towards agreed targets
- minutes of team meetings and standardisation activities
- list of resources (human and physical)
- records of communication with staff such as e-mails, memos, etc.
- records of giving support and advice to staff
- records of problems or critical incidents and actions taken
- written statements cross-referenced to the TAQA units' assessment criteria
- answers to questions issued by the awarding organisation
- records of discussions with your assessor.

Cross-referencing grid

This chapter contributes towards the following three TAQA IQA units' assessment criteria. Full details of the learning outcomes and assessment criteria for each TAQA unit can be found in the Appendices.

TAQA unit	Assessment criteria
Principles and practices of internally assuring the quality of assessment	2.1, 2.3 4.1 6.1, 6.3
Internally assuring the quality of assessment	1.1, 1.2 2.1, 2.2 3.1 4.1 5.1, 5.3, 5.4
Plan, allocate and monitor work	1.1, 1.2, 1.3, 1.4 2.1, 2.2 3.1, 3.2 4.1, 4.2

Theory focus

References and further information

Adair, J (2002) *John Adair's 100 Greatest Ideas for Effective Leadership and Management.* Mankato: Capstone.

Armstrong, M (2003) *A Handbook of Human Resource Management.* London: Kogan Page.

Armstrong, M (2008) *How To Be An Even Better Manager* (7th edition). London: Kogan Page.

Bacal, R (1998) *Performance Management.* New York: McGraw-Hill.

Belbin, M (2010) *Team Roles At Work* (2nd edition). Oxford: Butterworth-Heinemann.

Berne, E (1973) *Games People Play: The Psychology of Human Relationships.* London: Penguin Books.

Coverdale, R (1977) *Risk Thinking.* Bradford: The Coverdale Organisation.

Douglass, M and D (1993) *Manage Your Time, Your Work, Your Self.* New York: Amacom.

Friedman, M (1996) *Type A Behaviour: Its Diagnosis and Treatment.* New York: Plenum Press.

Gardner, H (1993) *Frames of Mind: Theory of Multiple Intelligences.* New York: Basic Books.

Handy, C and Constable, J (1988) *The Making of Managers.* London: Longman.

Honey, P (2001) *Improve Your People Skills* (2nd edition). London: CIPD.

Honey, P and Mumford, A (1986) *Manual of Learning Styles.* Coventry: Peter Honey Publications.

Kennedy, C (2007) *Guide to the Management Gurus* (5th edition). London: Random House.

Kermally, S (2002) Appraising Employee Performance. *Professional Manager,* 11(4): 30–31 July 2002.

Leitch, S (2006) *Review of Skills: Prosperity For All in the Global Economy; World Class Skills.* London: HM Treasury.

Mullins, LJ (2004) *Management and Organisational Behaviour* (7th edition). London: Prentice Hall.

Skinner, B F (1968) *The Technology of Teaching.* New York: Appleton, Century & Crofts.

Wallace, S and Gravells, J (2007) *Leadership and Leading Teams.* Exeter: Learning Matters.

Wallace, S and Gravells, J (2007) *Mentoring.* Exeter: Learning Matters.

Websites

Carl Jung: www.cgjungpage.org/

Gantt charts: www.mindtools.com/pages/article/newPPM_03.htm

Institute of Leadership and Management: www.i-l-m.com

Kiersey temperament theory: www.kiersey.com

Myers Briggs type indicator: www.myersbriggs.org

SWOT analysis: www.businessballs.com/swotanalysisfreetemplate.htm

Tuckman: www.infed.org/thinkers/tuckman.htm

Work plans: http://cec.vcn.bc.ca/cmp/modules/pm-pln.htm

UNIT 1: Understanding the principles and practices of assessment

LEVEL 3 (3 credits)

Learning outcomes The learner will:		Assessment criteria The learner can:
1. Understand the principles and requirements of assessment	1.1	Explain the function of assessment in learning and development
	1.2	Define the key concepts and principles of assessment
	1.3	Explain the responsibilities of the assessor
	1.4	Identify the regulations and requirements relevant to the assessment in own area of practice
2. Understand different types of assessment method	2.1	Compare the strengths and limitations of a range of assessment methods with reference to the needs of individual learners
3. Understand how to plan assessment	3.1	Summarise key factors to consider when planning assessment
	3.2	Evaluate the benefits of using a holistic approach to assessment
	3.3	Explain how to plan a holistic approach to assessment
	3.4	Summarise the types of risks that may be involved in assessment in own area of responsibility
	3.5	Explain how to minimise risks through the planning process
4. Understand how to involve learners and others in assessment	4.1	Explain the importance of involving the learner and others in the assessment process
	4.2	Summarise types of information that should be made available to learners and others involved in the assessment process
	4.3	Explain how peer and self-assessment can be used effectively to promote learner involvement and personal responsibility in the assessment of learning
	4.4	Explain how assessment arrangements can be adapted to meet the needs of individual learners

Learning outcomes The learner will:		Assessment criteria The learner can:
5. Understand how to make assessment decisions	5.1	Explain how to judge whether evidence is: • sufficient • authentic • current
	5.2	Explain how to ensure that assessment decisions are: • made against specified criteria • valid • reliable • fair
6. Understand quality assurance of the assessment process	6.1	Evaluate the importance of quality assurance in the assessment process
	6.2	Summarise quality assurance and standardisation procedures in own area of practice
	6.3	Summarise the procedures to follow when there are disputes concerning assessment in own area of practice
7. Understand how to manage information relating to assessment	7.1	Explain the importance of following procedures for the management of information relating to assessment
	7.2	Explain how feedback and questioning contribute to the assessment process
8. Understand the legal and good practice requirements in relation to assessment	8.1	Explain legal issues, policies and procedures relevant to assessment, including those for confidentiality, health, safety and welfare
	8.2	Explain the contribution that technology can make to the assessment process
	8.3	Evaluate requirements for equality and diversity and, where appropriate, bilingualism in relation to assessment
	8.4	Explain the value of reflective practice and continuing professional development in the assessment process

UNIT 2: Assess occupational competence in the work environment

LEVEL 3 (6 credits)

Learning outcomes The learner will:		Assessment criteria The learner can:
1. Be able to plan the assessment of occupational competence	1.1	Plan assessment of occupational competence based on the following methods: • observation of performance in the work environment • examining products of work • questioning the learner • discussing with the learner • use of others (witness testimony) • looking at learner statements • recognising prior learning
	1.2	Communicate the purpose, requirements and processes of assessing occupational competence to the learner
	1.3	Plan the assessment of occupational competence to address learner needs and current achievements
	1.4	Identify opportunities for holistic assessment
2. Be able to make assessment decisions about occupational competence	2.1	Use valid, fair and reliable assessment methods including: • observation of performance • examining products of work • questioning the learner • discussing with the learner • use of others (witness testimony) • looking at learner statements • recognising prior learning
	2.2	Make assessment decisions of occupational competence against specified criteria
	2.3	Follow standardisation procedures
	2.4	Provide feedback to learners that affirms achievement and identifies any further implications for learning, assessment and progression

Learning outcomes The learner will:		Assessment criteria The learner can:
3. Be able to provide required information following the assessment of occupational competence	3.1	Maintain records of the assessment of occupational competence, its outcomes and learner progress
	3.2	Make assessment information available to authorised colleagues
	3.3	Follow procedures to maintain the confidentiality of assessment information
4. Be able to maintain legal and good practice requirements when assessing occupational competence	4.1	Follow relevant policies, procedures and legislation for the assessment of occupational competence, including those for health, safety and welfare
	4.2	Apply requirements for equality and diversity and, where appropriate, bilingualism, when assessing occupational competence
	4.3	Evaluate own work in carrying out assessments of occupational competence
	4.4	Maintain the currency of own expertise and competence as relevant to own role in assessing occupational competence

UNIT 3: Assess vocational skills, knowledge and understanding

LEVEL 3 (6 credits)

Learning outcomes The learner will:		Assessment criteria The learner can:
1. Be able to prepare assessments of vocational skills, knowledge and understanding	1.1	Select methods to assess vocational skills, knowledge and understanding which address learner needs and meet assessment requirements, including: ● assessments of the learner in simulated environments ● skills tests ● oral and written questions ● assignments ● projects ● case studies ● recognising prior learning
	1.2	Prepare resources and conditions for the assessment of vocational skills, knowledge and understanding
	1.3	Communicate the purpose, requirements and processes of assessment of vocational skills, knowledge and understanding to learners
2. Be able to carry out assessments of vocational skills, knowledge and understanding	2.1	Manage assessments of vocational skills, knowledge and understanding to meet assessment requirements
	2.2	Provide support to learners within agreed limitations
	2.3	Analyse evidence of learner achievement
	2.4	Make assessment decisions relating to vocational skills, knowledge and understanding against specified criteria
	2.5	Follow standardisation procedures
	2.6	Provide feedback to the learner that affirms achievement and identifies any further implications for learning, assessment and progression

Learning outcomes The learner will:		Assessment criteria The learner can:
3. Be able to provide required Information following the assessment of vocational skills, knowledge and understanding	3.1	Maintain records of the assessment of vocational skills, knowledge and understanding, its outcomes and learner progress
	3.2	Make assessment information available to authorised colleagues as required
	3.3	Follow procedures to maintain the confidentiality of assessment information
4. Be able to maintain legal and good practice requirements when assessing vocational skills, knowledge and understanding	4.1	Follow relevant policies, procedures and legislation relating to the assessment of vocational skills, knowledge and understanding, including those for health, safety and welfare
	4.2	Apply requirements for equality and diversity and, where appropriate, bilingualism
	4.3	Evaluate own work in carrying out assessments of vocational skills, knowledge and understanding
	4.4	Take part in continuing professional development to ensure current expertise and competence in assessing vocational skills, knowledge and understanding

UNIT 4: Understanding the principles and practices of internally assuring the quality of assessment

LEVEL 4 (6 credits)

Learning outcomes The learner will:		Assessment criteria The learner can:
1. Understand the context and principles of internal quality assurance	1.1	Explain the functions of internal quality assurance in learning and development
	1.2	Explain the key concepts and principles of the internal quality assurance of assessment
	1.3	Explain the roles of practitioners involved in the internal and external quality assurance process
	1.4	Explain the regulations and requirements for internal quality assurance in own area of practice
2. Understand how to plan the internal quality assurance of assessment	2.1	Evaluate the importance of planning and preparing internal quality assurance activities
	2.2	Explain what an internal quality assurance plan should contain
	2.3	Summarise the preparations that need to be made for internal quality assurance, including: • information collection • communications • administrative arrangements • resources
3. Understand techniques and criteria for monitoring the quality of assessment internally	3.1	Evaluate different techniques for sampling evidence of assessment, including use of technology
	3.2	Explain the appropriate criteria to use for judging the quality of the assessment process
4. Understand how to internally maintain and improve the quality of assessment	4.1	Summarise the types of feedback, support and advice that assessors may need to maintain and improve the quality of assessment
	4.2	Explain standardisation requirements in relation to assessment
	4.3	Explain relevant procedures regarding disputes about the quality of assessment

Learning outcomes The learner will:		Assessment criteria The learner can:
5. Understand how to manage information relevant to the internal quality assurance of assessment	5.1	Evaluate requirements for information management, data protection and confidentiality in relation to the internal quality assurance of assessment
6. Understand the legal and good practice requirements for the internal quality assurance of assessment	6.1	Evaluate legal issues, policies and procedures relevant to the internal quality assurance of assessment, including those for health, safety and welfare
	6.2	Evaluate different ways in which technology can contribute to the internal quality assurance of assessment
	6.3	Explain the value of reflective practice and continuing professional development in relation to internal quality assurance
	6.4	Evaluate requirements for equality and diversity and, where appropriate, bilingualism, in relation to the internal quality assurance of assessment

UNIT 5: Internally assure the quality of assessment

LEVEL 4 (6 credits)

Learning outcomes The learner will:		Assessment criteria The learner can:
1. Plan the internal quality assurance of assessment	1.1	Plan monitoring activities according to the requirements of own role
	1.2	Make arrangements for internal monitoring activities to assure quality
2. Internally evaluate the quality of assessment	2.1	Carry out internal monitoring activities to quality requirements
	2.2	Evaluate assessor expertise and competence in relation to the requirements of their role
	2.3	Evaluate the planning and preparation of assessment processes
	2.4	Determine whether assessment methods are safe, fair, valid and reliable
	2.5	Determine whether assessment decisions are made using the specified criteria
	2.6	Compare assessor decisions to ensure they are consistent
3. Internally maintain and improve the quality of assessment	3.1	Provide assessors with feedback, advice and support, including professional development opportunities, which help them to maintain and improve the quality of assessment
	3.2	Apply procedures to standardise assessment practices and outcomes
4. Manage information relevant to the internal quality assurance of assessment	4.1	Apply procedures for recording, storing and reporting information relating to internal quality assurance
	4.2	Follow procedures to maintain confidentiality of internal quality assurance information

Learning outcomes The learner will:		Assessment criteria The learner can:
5. Maintain legal and good practice requirements when internally monitoring and maintaining the quality of assessment	5.1	Apply relevant policies, procedures and legislation in relation to internal quality assurance, including those for health, safety and welfare
	5.2	Apply requirements for equality and diversity and, where appropriate, bilingualism, in relation to internal quality assurance
	5.3	Critically reflect on own practice in internally assuring the quality of assessment
	5.4	Maintain the currency of own expertise and competence in internally assuring the quality of assessment

UNIT 6: Plan, allocate and monitor work in own area of responsibility

LEVEL 4 (5 credits)

Learning outcomes The learner will:		Assessment criteria The learner can:
1. Produce a work plan for own area of responsibility	1.1	Explain the context in which work is to be undertaken
	1.2	Identify the skills base and the resources available
	1.3	Examine priorities and success criteria needed for the team
	1.4	Produce a work plan for own area of responsibility
2. Allocate and agree responsibilities with team members	2.1	Identify team members' responsibilities for identified work activities
	2.2	Agree responsibilities and SMART (*Specific, Measurable, Achievable, Realistic and Time-bound*) objectives with team members
3. Monitor the progress and quality of work in own area of responsibility and provide feedback	3.1	Identify ways to monitor progress and quality of work
	3.2	Monitor and evaluate progress against agreed standards and provide feedback to team members
4. Review and amend plans of work for own area of responsibility and communicate changes	4.1	Review and amend work plan where changes are needed
	4.2	Communicate changes to team members